A *Lady* IN THE MID-MORNING SUN

ANGIE MILAN CRUZ

PAGE PUBLISHING
Conneaut Lake, PA

First originally published by Page Publishing 2024

ISBN 979-8-89315-924-0 (pbk)
ISBN 979-8-89315-945-5 (digital)

Printed in the United States of America

Chapter 1

A lady in her midforties with short black hair and piercing blue eyes decided to conduct her morning rituals near the National Park when she had time to run. She liked spending family time near Beverly's favorite place, Shoshone Point, sometimes around the South Rim near the Colorado River to stretch, and the outer parts of Grand Canyon National Park, where it was easier for her not to get lost.

Beverly's not afraid of heights, so it was easier for her to concentrate on her routine.

As Beverly did her daily stretching, watching the sun rise in the mist, she found it thrilling each morning as she jogged near the park.

Amongst the many rock formations, rocky trails, natural animal life, and plants, Beverly watched the sun slowly creep near the mountaintop that she always found so breathtaking during her routine. Watching the colors pop from one cliff to another was admired by millions who visited the park yearly, including the Descanti-Cartwright family.

Beverly was reluctant that day to run through the park because it had rained the previous night.

She wouldn't walk or jog through the park out of fear of torrential rain. Around the springtime, heavy downfalls happen almost every year; she went anyway. This time Beverly decided to run down a road familiar to her near the canyon.

It was odd for her. Beverly felt that if she didn't stick to her morning rituals, she was missing out.

Beverly saw a few couples whom she bumped into several times during her runs through the park. She noticed one couple bickering about moving from Arizona to Virginia.

She was good with details. The female was around twenty-two, five-foot-four-inch tall, and curvy. Kathy was born and raised in Arizona. She wasn't saying anything. Her boyfriend was practically yelling at Kathy about moving away. It was more like a verbal conversation than a heated discussion between Kathy and Derrick. There were no signs or red flags that Derrick was abusive. Kathy had the right kind of skills to speak with Derrick.

Her boyfriend, Derrick, sometimes wasn't good at expressing his feelings. Men usually don't know how to do the simplest things, like express what they feel. He looked around twenty-four, five-foot-eleven-inch tall, and had a slim build. Derrick's parents moved from New Jersey to Arizona. Derrick was about twelve years old when he moved with his parents to Arizona.

Beverly noticed two elderly couples, originally from Santa Fe, in their late fifties, just walking and picking up rocks for their collection. They were geologists from the University of Arizona. Every year around springtime, they would gather rocks to study them with their students.

So Beverly continued pacing herself in the park. She didn't think anything of it. She went on to finish her morning ritual and then headed to her car.

As Beverly was sitting in the car, she noticed through the rearview mirror that the couple was still debating about moving. Beverly remained there, sitting in her 2021 Buick Luxury SUV. Jonathan Sr. had just bought it for Beverly a month before Christmas. She sat there for a moment to watch. She decided to call her husband, Jonathan Sr., to talk about the couple. Kathy and Derrick were still having a little disagreement about moving to Virginia.

Jonathan Sr. told Beverly to just keep an eye on both of them, just in case. Jonathan Sr. was on the other side of the park, conducting his tour with four other junior rangers and guests in the park.

After finishing her conversation with Jonathan Sr. about the couple, she saw Derrick and Kathy proceed to their individual cars and speed out, going in different directions.

Beverly seemed relieved that the couple left and went their separate ways to cool off without incident.

Derrick was offered a job as a corporate attorney for a medical facility in Williamsburg, Virginia. He graduated with honors. His future fiancée works as a medical provider at the Planned Parenthood Clinic for Women's Health and Mental Health Services in Arizona after college.

Kathy loved helping her community with the necessary services that Planned Parenthood had to offer, so she had no plans to move.

Both were successful and respected in their fields. It seemed Derrick wanted to start fresh in a different location, but she wasn't ready to move across the US.

Beverly was a stay-at-home mom who was a cancer survivor in waiting, raising three children while her husband, Jonathan Sr., worked as a veteran park ranger near the same area where Beverly went to do her morning rituals.

Beverly and Jonathan Sr.'s kids were cared for by a nanny in her early sixties with a smile that lit up the entire room. Mrs. Daniels enjoyed taking care of Tammy, who was fourteen. Jonathan Jr. was ten, and Genny was eight. She was hired to mind her beautiful children during Beverly's chemo two years before.

They also had two grown children in college—Matthew and Jennifer.

Jonathan Sr. and Beverly had hired Mrs. Daniels to stay working for an infinite length of time. She was doing a remarkable job with their kids in their lovely five-bedroom, two-and-a-half-bathroom countryside home. They raised chickens, two horses, and a pony since her grown kids were tykes.

Mrs. Daniel had a master's degree in child development services and a master's in childcare. Her children, Robert and Jacklyn, were grown up and in college.

Robert was at a university studying for his master's in child development and psychology, just like his mom did in 1984, and Jacklyn was studying criminal law.

Jonathan Cartwright Sr. and Beverly Descanti were from well-to-do families in Arizona. Both of their parents were immigrants to the US in the early nineteenth century. Beverly's parents and grandparents were from a small town in Palermo, Italy. Jonathan Sr.'s parents and grandparents were from the city of Glasgow, Scotland, with a population of 640,000 residents, a whist away from Edinburgh.

The following day, Beverly was walking like she always did. It wasn't like she was being nosy. It was like she was picked by God to watch over them. She overheard Kathy and Derrick arguing about moving and having a family—the same conversation, twice during her walk.

Derrick was relentless, while Kathy was passive about moving. It seemed that the couple wasn't budging at all. Beverly heard Kathy say to Derrick, "Wasn't we planning to start a family of our own right here in Flagstaff?"

Beverly knew them only because of their in-fighting with each other during those two encounters. Every time she saw the couple, it was about the same thing. Derrick was straightforward and wasn't violent. Derrick had the tendency to raise his voice when he talked. He talked a lot with his hands. Kathy, on the other hand, was docile and shy. It bothered her a lot because she was always in front of the other guests visiting the park.

No one got involved because it was only small tiffs. There is nothing more than that. One of the guests said out loud, "Couples debating is normal."

One morning, Beverly saw Kathy alone, just sitting on a large boulder, looking up. The sky above her was clear but a little humid. This time, it was a little different. Kathy was alone, without Derrick.

Beverly didn't dare ask Kathy how she was feeling or ask about Derrick. It was like Beverly knew them and wanted to help. Beverly respected Kathy's private time. Kathy kind of hinted with a glance, so Beverly just went about her business. Beverly, as usual, stayed in her place to avoid any further awkwardness.

She felt uneasy. She was worried that Kathy was dealing with this back-and-forth with Derrick entirely alone.

Assuming that her family was as worried as she was, just leaving her family and her career was very scary for Kathy, who lived in Arizona her entire life.

Kathy never traveled alone or with Derrick outside her hometown, only on family trips with their own families. She knew her neighbors very well. Kathy felt more comfortable staying in Arizona than moving somewhere else, like Virginia.

Derrick did have some family members in Williamsburg. Derrick was going to be okay there. Kathy wasn't okay with it. She knew Derrick's cousins and aunt only through phone calls and video chats on Messenger. They were all encouraging Kathy to move to Virginia. She wasn't going unless she was willing to leave Arizona for good. That wasn't in her plans. Derrick at first, but now his plans changed when he was offered a job.

The same day she saw Kathy, Jonathan Sr. and Beverly meet up to run that weekend. Jonathan Sr. was starting his vacation in a few days. The couple made vacation plans to take their family to Bush Gardens in Florida and then to Universal Studios.

It was their first time ever going to Universal Studios. They were anticipating going. Jonathan Sr. made all the reservations ahead of time with his wife and all their kids. They were all very excited to go.

Meanwhile, Beverly was concerned about her upcoming visit with her oncologist. It was scheduled for the following week. She wanted to attend. She had been in remission for a couple of months now.

During her first diagnosis of second-stage breast cancer in April 2022, Beverly's fear of dying or losing her full body and curly hair was on her mind. Everyone complimented her beautiful hair all the time. She was one of many who didn't die or lose any hair before, during, or after treatment. She was grateful for that.

Her progress looked very promising, according to Dr. Kingston. Dr. Prisilla Kingston made plans to reschedule Beverly's oncology appointment so she can spend some time with her parents during her vacation in Florida.

The Kingstons came from a long line of oncologists—her father, Dr. Tim Kingston, and her uncle Kevin, who was also an oncologist till he fell ill twelve years earlier with onset dementia.

They ran a small private clinic alongside Prisilla's cousin, Samantha, and his daughter, Prisilla, with close to forty years of experience in oncology altogether.

The Kingstons were loved in the community for saving countless lives from various types of cancer.

Both brothers, Tim and Kevin, were huge donors at the HealthCare Hospital/Grand Canyon in Arizona.

As young resident students at North Country, Tim and Kevin were the first to be invited to work with Doctors Without Borders in Zambia, Indonesia, and some parts of South America.

They were known for their non-profit work and contributions and were recognized by their high honors for achievements in oncology.

The Kingston family had a success rate of 82 percent. The Kingstons had been loved by their patients for many years. Many, to this day, are in remission, or any new diagnosis of cancer is well taken care of.

They were well-received by the community. The lives they couldn't save were remembered in a big way. They were recognized by the American Cancer Society.

There were foundations in development for those who passed away with cancer.

The year before, Tim's wife passed away from a heart attack at a young age. Tim never remarried. Tim remained faithful till he met a new girl. Three years after Deborah's death, he dated a woman named Maggie.

Tim's children didn't like his girlfriend very much. She was a gold digger for some members of the community in her hometown of Flagstaff. Tim seemed happy, so Prisilla, Gigi, and Bernard were happy for their dad. After the death of their mom, it was hard for them.

It took a few years to accept their mom's passing. Deborah was the queen of the family. Every year, they all celebrated Deborah's life with balloons and candles to illuminate her fascinating soul.

She was very pretty, bright, and loved to cook. She was a school principal at a private high school in Arizona for seventeen years before her sudden death from a heart attack.

Deborah was voted the Best Principal of the Year by her peers because of her charismatic and charming spirit. She was admired by all the parents, her students, and faculty members across the board.

Tim and Deborah were also childhood sweethearts and enjoyed their time together even when Tim had to work long hours. They would communicate during the day. They were together on his day off from work and traveling with his wife, Deborah, when possible.

The Kingston and the Hollywell also had two other children—Gigi and Bernard. They both had just started college when their mom passed away. They grew up living their lives in different parts of the US. Gigi and Bernard made plans to return to Flagstaff after graduation. Every holiday, the Hollywell-Kinston family would gather together to spend time.

Two days later, the Descanti-Cartwright family was getting their suitcases ready for their trip to Florida. Their grown kids, Matthew and Jennifer, were going to meet up with their family during spring break. Beverly, Jonathan Sr., and the grandparents of Matthew, Jennifer, Tammy, Jonathan Jr., and Genny were traveling as a whole family. They hadn't seen their adult children in a couple of years since they left for CalTech and UCLA in California (fictional students).

The Descanti and Cartwright families were very close. It was like it was meant to be. They were all respected for their way of handling things without arguing in front of people.

It wasn't strange that they got along so well. Their morals, values, and respect were equally shared. They all knew that family was essential, without a doubt, rememberable, and very familiar.

Weeks later, Derrick split up for a few months because of their riff about moving to Virginia. His new job in Williamsburg would start soon. Kathy and Derrick decided to separate for a few months so Derrick could start his new career. Kathy remained in Arizona to continue her path in nursing with planned parenthood. She would be starting some additional classes to become a supervising registered nurse.

They both agreed to have a long-distance relationship for a few months. It was hard to be separated from Derrick. They were junior high school sweethearts and had known each other's family since they were adolescents. They had been together for almost ten years without any separation between them.

Derrick was one and a half years older than Kathy; they looked good together. Even the Gerber and Villanueva families knew that they would be great together as a couple. Kathy and Derrick were ambitious. They aimed to become successful with work, family, relationships, and kids of their own one day.

They were middle-class families with small businesses. Flagstaff community members made them heroes for their bravery and being humanitarians.

Mr. Charles Villanueva prevented an assailant from robbing the store. Mr. Villanueva was a part-time martial arts teacher. Charles was a single parent to Kathy after his ex-wife, Dedee, ran off with another man. Charles decided to take Dedee to court for full custody of Kathy when she was nine.

The judge ruled in his favor because he was able to support Kathy with love and finances. Kathy would be better off there than being with her mom, Dedee, who wasn't employed. Dedee didn't have stable housing for Kathy, so Judge Pickman granted Charles full custody of Kathy.

Judge Pickman gave her enough time for Dedee to find employment. Dedee had to be stable between six months and a year before the judge would revisit the case and possibly grant shared custody amongst the Villanuevas.

She said to herself that after a year, she would be able to be around her daughter. Dedee was thrilled about the idea. She worked hard to maintain stability and employment to help Kathy financially.

They eventually coparented Kathy and lived separate lives. Charles had been dating for a while, but there was nothing concrete.

He was more focused on his business, his part-time work as a martial arts instructor, and his daughter Kathy. Then he met Veronica.

Mr. Victor and Janet Gerber saved the life of an employee who was choking while eating lunch in the back space of his business.

Mr. Gerber and his wife, Janet, were loved by community members for their endless work. Their work with a foundation for underprivileged and military kids who have lost a male parent in Afghanistan since 2013. The ones who were married got all the veteran benefits from their deceased husbands. Unfortunately, the ones who weren't married or engaged missed out on the benefits. The men's family who lost a loved one did get full military honors on their behalf.

Their struggles were real. The community was behind them with all kinds of support, food, housing, and guidance, as needed. The kids' parents, who needed the help, got the support they needed, while their moms worked one to two jobs to support their children. Even that wasn't enough at times.

They were able to get donations from the community. Meals were prepared for the kids while being supervised by Miss Janet. The donations they received were a huge help for those family members.

Chapter 2

BEVERLY'S REMISSION/ JONATHAN SR.'S PROMOTION

After their fabulous trip to Bush Gardens and Universal Studio, Beverly got a reminder that she had an appointment with Dr. Prisilla Kingston for blood work. Dr. Prisilla Kingston secured an appointment with the radiologist for an MRI exam and screening.

Beverly continued getting better. She wasn't experiencing any problems, which is a good sign. She wasn't as tired as she was months before. Her chemotherapy sessions were a bitch, but she remained optimistic.

Matthew and Jennifer went to Arizona with their parents for the remainder of spring break. In five days, they would be returning to school to finish their second and third years at the university.

Jonathan Sr. was anxious about Beverly's upcoming appointment with Dr. Kingston. He's been with Beverly and all five of their kids since day one. He was a hard worker. He was also being considered for a promotion but didn't know when it was going to occur.

He'd been a veteran park ranger for nineteen plus years and was not even ready to retire. Jonathan Sr. was the primary breadwinner. He had been ready for this promotion and a higher salary for some time. He earned it. Every day for the past nineteen years, he kept the park safe for visitors.

What saved him from financial disaster was his grown kids, Matthew and Jennifer, getting full scholarships to attend Cal-Tech and UCLA without added expenses.

Before Beverly was diagnosed with stage two breast cancer, she was a paralegal for about ten years at a law firm. Beverly needed to attend to her health, and Jonathan Sr. agreed with his wife's decision.

Her supervisor gave Beverly enough time to heal before returning to work if she desired to do so.

Matthew and Jennifer were super proud of their mom's recovery. She was able to stay calm throughout her diagnosis. Her success with her cancer treatment was refreshing and powerful.

All her kids and her husband, Jonathan Sr., were her biggest fans through it all. Although her youngest kids didn't understand, they were encouraged by her unwavering strength. She was at ease with the kids adapting and being kids.

Tammy, Jonathan Jr., and Genny were very supportive and strong in their own impressionable ways.

Beverly was into health and fitness, as were Matthew and Jennifer. They would jog with their mom before they left for college, and they also included meditation and yoga. Matthew was more into jogging and weightlifting, while Jennifer was into meditation and yoga like her mom.

Jonathan Sr. was also a weight lifter since he was a teenager, way into adulthood. He was in remarkable shape and continued to do so because of his work.

Tammy, Jonathan Jr., and Genny were on their way to becoming images of their older siblings and parents, Jonathan Sr. and Beverly.

All their kids were well-mannered and polite. They behaved well around other people. Jonathan Sr. was strict, but he was an excellent dad and was equally fair to all his kids.

Beverly loved her family. She would do anything to keep her family very close to her bosom. Beverly and Jonathan Sr. got the same treatment from their parents and passed it on to their children. They were equally fair, loving, strict, and well-mannered.

In a few days, Beverly was preparing for her appointment with Dr. Kingston. She was not worried about it. She had been following the doctor's orders so far, so she wasn't expecting any bad news. Even if she did, she is prepared for the unexpected.

Three days later, spring break was over. Mrs. Daniels arrived at the Descanti-Cartwright residence to get the kids ready for school. Beverly was getting ready for her oncology appointment with Dr. Prisilla Kingston at 10:15 a.m.

Jonathan Sr. kissed his wife and his kids before heading to work. He greeted Mrs. Daniel briskly. Mrs. Daniel greeted Mr. Cartwright. Her infectious smile always lit up a room every time she walked in.

Mrs. Daniels and Beverly had enough time to prepare the kids' lunch along with snacks. Beverly was very meticulous about what Tammy, Jonathan Jr., and Genny consumed every day.

While Beverly waited with her kids for the school bus to arrive, Mrs. Daniels went upstairs and made the kids' beds. She then placed a load of laundry in the washing machine in the basement.

After the beds were made and the laundry was in the dryer, Beverly and Mrs. Daniels sat briefly to chat, sipping on some herbal blueberry tea.

Beverly spoke about her appreciation for Mrs. Daniels. She told Mrs. Daniel that she was considering giving her a slight raise for all the help she provided for her and the kids, Tammy, Jonathan Jr., and Genny.

For a moment, Mrs. Daniels looked teary-eyed and returned the courtesy to Ms. Descanti. They both smiled and continued sipping their cup of tea.

After three years of working for the Descanti-Cartwright family, she had treated Mrs. Daniels like a family member. The kids adored her very much. Jonathan Sr. and Beverly were really impressed with Mrs. Daniels and her experience with kids.

Half an hour later, Mrs. Daniel accompanied Beverly to her oncology appointment.

As they were driving through town with the morning glare of the sun beaming into the car, they lowered the visors. They laughed when they put the visors down at the same time.

Mrs. Daniel asked. "Are you okay?"

Beverly responded with a smile, "Yes, I am," and went on talking about the plans for the day after seeing Dr. Kingston.

They arrived at the Kingston Clinic. It was about a ten-mile drive from the Descanti-Cartwright home. It made it easier for Beverly to get there without any issues, unless there was traffic.

Beverly parked the car, and they both went inside.

The front receptionist greeted Beverly and Mrs. Daniels as they walked in and asked them to have a seat.

Beverly seemed a little nervous. Mrs. Daniels patted her hand and said, "Beverly, you are a strong woman, and I am here to support you."

"We are women, and we must stick together," Beverly said, smirking. After that, her nervousness seized like a weight lifted from her shoulders.

Dr. Prisilla Kingston was just coming out of her office when she saw Beverly. She greeted her and Mrs. Daniels.

Dr. Kingston escorted Beverly to her office. They sat and caught up. Beverly talked about her and the entire family's trip to Bush Garden and Universal Studios.

Dr. Kingston just came from a medical convention in Thailand thirty hours earlier. Beverly gave some souvenirs to Prisilla from her family trip. Dr. Kingston was thankful, and they went on talking.

Dr. Kingston explained that she was going to conduct some blood work and a routine breast checkup. A nurse came into Dr. Kingston's office and asked Beverly to follow her to the lab for blood work.

Seven minutes later, she returned to Dr. Kingston's office to get her breast examined. After that, Dr. Kingston talked a little about her MRI. She told Beverly that if she had any questions, she should not hesitate to ask. Beverly relied on Dr. Kingston because she was one of the best oncologists in Arizona. Regarding Beverly's ongoing health issues, they were well under control. She trusted her with her life.

Once they finished, Dr. Kingston escorted Beverly to the front desk to schedule her next oncology appointment.

Beverly and Mrs. Daniel left and headed to her car. They ran some errands along the way. They went to Walmart to buy fruits, yogurt, and vegetables for Beverly's dietary cleansing. They also bought some extra things for Jonathan Sr. and the kids. Mrs. Daniel bought some items to take home once she had finished her chores at the Descanti-Cartwright home.

Meanwhile, Jonathan Sr. was about to hear some good news about his promotion and raise. His supervisor, Miguel, called Jonathan Sr. to his office. They talked about family and work for twenty minutes. Miguel told Jonathan Sr. about how valuable he was. Miguel was excited to provide Jonathan Sr. with the good news.

Jonathan Sr. couldn't contain himself. It was much-needed news for his family. He was so consumed with Beverly's diagnosis that it took up a lot of his energy. Secretly, without worrying Beverly, she should only be focusing on regaining her strength and her health. Jonathan Sr. didn't show too much of his emotions, but they were on the surface.

Then Miguel gave Jonathan Sr. the good news. Miguel congratulated Jonathan Sr. and shook his hands. Not only did Jonathan Sr. get a raise of $47,000 more a year, but he also got a $5,000 bonus. Jonathan Sr. was now the new director of parks and recreation, as well as supervising a team of thirty staff members.

Jonathan Sr. was so excited. He had taken a moment to turn away from Miguel to digest the good news. Miguel congratulated Jonathan Sr. again and gave him his new title and shield.

Miguel told Jonathan Sr. to take the remaining day off to be with his family. Jonathan Sr. called his parents to come over to their home. He said he would explain more and wanted to share his good fortune with his entire family.

They lived about 2,240 miles from Phoenix to the downtown Flagstaff/Grand Canyon area. His parents, Jonathan I and Yolanda, told their son that they would need some time to prepare a suitcase and an overnight bag to spend a night or two. Jonathan Sr. said it was fine. His parents would visit in a day or two.

Jonathan Sr. didn't say anything till everyone was gathered. Jonathan Sr. was going to Skype Matthew and Jennifer to share the news when everyone was present. The family knew their schedule, so it was perfect timing to share the good news once his parents arrived.

Jonathan Sr. called Beverly to ask about her appointment with Dr. Kingston. She said, "Everything went well. Dr. Prisilla Kingston is waiting for my blood work to return from Q Diagnostics." She also mentioned to Jonathan Sr. that her next visit with the radiology MRI exam would be in three weeks. He was worried but was relieved.

He wanted to tell Beverly about the good news. He refrained from spilling the beans about his promotion till the whole family got together. He told Beverly that his parents were coming for a visit in a few days. She loved his parents coming over. They always had interesting stories to tell.

Beverly told Jonathan Sr. in return that she would like to invite her parents to come over. Jonathan Sr. said, "Absolutely, honey. Your parents were a hoot." Jonathan Sr. loved them as much as Beverly loved his parents.

The Descant-Cartwright family made up the guest rooms for both of their parents and bought food and their favorite wines and cognac. Jonathan I and his wife, Yolanda Cartwright, were Jonathan Sr.'s parents, and Antonio and Sofia Descanti were Beverly's parents.

Beverly, Mrs. Daniel, and Jonathan Sr. prepared potato and macaroni salads, seasoned the beef brisket, and prepared baked ziti and the kids' favorite meal—antipasto, baked mac and cheese, tiramisu, and assorted baked pies for the next day.

Beverly was on a strict diet. Beverly seasoned a skinless chicken, baked potatoes with chives, and prepared a power green salad for her. Tammy walked in, got herself a bottle of water from the fridge, and headed back to her room. Tammy always did her homework, so she could have the whole weekend only to do her chores.

Jonathan Sr. asked Mrs. Daniels if she would be honored to attend his family get-together on Saturday. He added, "You have been by Beverly's side since her diagnosis. We consider you like family."

She said, "I can come for a few hours, then I have to leave because my sister, Robin, is coming to town to see me."

Jonathan Sr. and Beverly said, "It's fine. If you can't come, we will understand."

Mrs. Daniels said she would come. She wanted to help with setting up the dining room table.

They both nodded their heads with glee. "We will appreciate any help you can provide us. We will assure you some compensation."

Mrs. Daniels said, "It would be my pleasure. Don't worry about money. Remember, I am family. Family doesn't charge family." Jonathan Sr. placed his hand over his chest and said thank you.

Beverly told Mrs. Daniels to take the day off on Friday so Mrs. Daniels could rest. Saturday would be a day of food, fun, drink, and something else that would have to wait till Saturday. She smiled like she always did. The Descanti-Cartwright family was very happy to have her as a nanny. After that, Mrs. Daniels left for the day.

The kids finished taking their baths and got into their pajamas. Beverly and Jonathan Sr. kissed their kids on the foreheads and went upstairs to their rooms. Tammy and Genny slept in the same room, while Jonathan Jr. had his own room.

Tammy would be fifteen in September. She told her mom on different occasions that she needed a little space for herself. Her parents told Tammy many times that they would figure it out after she turned sixteen.

Jonathan Sr. and Beverly sat in the living room. They watched one of their all-time favorite movies, *Prime Video*, hugged and kissed each other, and headed to bed after the movie finished.

Their sexual life was on pause. Jonathan Sr. was in love with Beverly, and the feeling was mutual. Jonathan Sr. understood that Beverly's health was a priority over making love to each other.

He felt happy just to hold his wife close to his buff body. She was in love with Jonathan Sr. too. They were fine just being around each other. Until Beverly was strong enough to make love to her first love, he was extremely content with how things were then.

As she was dozing off to sleep, he lay on his back, looking up at the ceiling, thinking about how he was going to share the good news with his family. He was an excellent planner. He slowly started to fall asleep, turned to Beverly, and put his arm around her.

Every night, he would do the same because that was how she rested comfortably. Knowing that Jonathan Sr. was there was good enough for Bev.

Jonathan Sr. slept in for a little bit longer. Beverly was awake, got her kids ready for their morning weekend walk, and headed to the nearby park. Their beds were made. One day out of the week, the kids were responsible for cleaning their rooms as needed. Mrs. Daniel came a few hours later. Mrs. Daniels was invited as a guest to "Jonathan Sr.'s Good News."

Beverly took a day off from her routine to enjoy a day with her children. The kids were excited and already hyped so early in the morning. Beverly felt complete seeing her children happy, healthy, and playing. Doing their own thing was splendor to her heart.

Genny was the little clown in the group. She always made everyone laugh with her sweet tactics. Tammy was very shy but loved her gymnastics, so the park was ideal for her to practice, while Jonathan Jr. always enjoyed playing video games and basketball.

When it came to Jonathan Jr. playing video games, she only allowed him to play for an hour after homework was done and an hour and a half on Sunday. Saturday was family day, unless Jonathan Sr. had to work over the weekend. That was their routine. Every weekend, Beverly managed to create activities for Tammy, Jonathan Jr., and Genny to stay sharp.

Beverly loaded the kids in the car and headed to the park for a couple of hours. It was 8:00 a.m., so they had plenty of time to get ready for the family get-together later in the afternoon.

Jonathan Sr.'s parents were going to arrive at around 3:30 p.m. Beverly's parents lived nearby, so they weren't rushing to get there till Jonathan Sr.'s parents were already there.

Jonathan Sr. finally got up, went to the bathroom to do his morning rituals, went downstairs to make coffee, sat in the kitchen nook, and listened to an audiobook while Beverly was in the park with their kids.

Jonathan Sr. was reminiscing, reading, and contemplating how the day would go. He wanted everything to be as perfect as possible.

His signature beef brisket was going into the oven in an hour. It took him at least seven to eight hours to slow-cook it. The family loved his beef brisket. It was flavorful and tasty, and it melted in your mouth.

Everything else was already prepared and ready to hit the oven later in the day.

Mrs. Daniels called Beverly and then Jonathan Sr. to let them know that she'd be arriving around 2:30 p.m. to help. They were okay with it and in accord.

The table was all set the night before, so that was one less thing to do. Beverly had covered the table with her favorite tablecloth. The table was all set up fabulously. The day was going to be an exciting one, especially for Jonathan Sr.'s family when they heard the news about his promotion.

Beverly and the kids came back from the park at around 11:30 a.m. Tammy, Jonathan Jr., and Genny got their things ready for the family gathering later on. Tammy and Genny had their own bathroom, and Jonathan Jr. would use the shower he and Matthew shared.

Mrs. Daniel just arrived on time and started helping Jonathan Sr. and Beverly in the kitchen while the kids were watching TV quietly.

Jonathan Jr. wanted to play video games, but Beverly reminded him that he had enough time on the screen at the park. "Just keep your sisters' company," she said, so he did.

Then the bell rang, and they were Jonathan Sr.'s parents, Yolanda and Jonathan I. They greeted their only son at the door. Only Beverly and Jonathan Sr. were allowed to open the front door.

He was so happy to see them. He was glad that they came casually. It was not a formal event but just a get-together. His parents tend to overdress. His dad was a marine, so the dress code was up to par. His mom, on the other hand, was always dressed daintily.

By the echoes at the entrance of their home, Beverly heard them come in. Beverly provided a warm hug to Jonathan Sr.'s parents, smiled, and they all went to the kitchen. His dad was heading to the living room to greet his grandchildren; Jonathan Sr. followed. Then Yolanda grabbed her babies and gave them a group hug.

Mrs. Daniels said hello and continued helping in the kitchen. Yolanda asked if they needed any help. Beverly responded, "Momma Yolanda, just take it easy. You are here to spend time with us." Beverly said to Yolanda that her mom, Sofia, and her dad, Antonio, would be coming soon. Yolanda Cartwright was gleaming when she heard that Sofia would be there. They were about the same age and got along very well from day one, when their kids became bf/gf in private school.

While the kids sat between their dad and granddad in the living room, Genny was dancing to her favorite tunes on YouTube TV. They loved watching Genny dance her little heart out. She was quite a dancer.

Beverly's parents called to say that they were just ten minutes away. Beverly was happy that they were coming too. She wasn't going to share anything about her appointment with Dr. Kingston till she was sure that she had good news to tell them. Bev knew her parents would press her to say what happened at her appointment with Dr. Kingston.

Beverly called out to everyone in the kitchen that her parents would be there shortly. Everyone said okay at the same time and laughed. You could hear Genny saying, "You owe me a pizza."

Then Beverly's parents arrived. The kids ran and gave them a big hug and a kiss, then ran back to the living room.

The ladies chatted in the kitchen, putting baked mac and cheese, baked potatoes, and ziti in the oven. The beef brisket was just about fully cooked. It smelled wonderful, just the way Jonathan Sr. made it so many times before.

Beverly's father, Antonio, went to join the men and the kids in the living room till dinner was done.

Shaking and patting each other's shoulders, the men also got along so well. They were military men—hard-core and headstrong.

About forty-five to fifty minutes later, everything was done. Beverly asked the kids to wash their hands and head to the dining room once they were done. Jonathan Sr. removed the cover off the Dutch oven pot, and everyone practically drooled from the smell of beef brisket.

After that, Beverly, Sofia, Yolanda, and Mrs. Daniels started bringing in the bakeware to the dining room, went back to the kitchen to get everything else, and set it on the dining room table. The table was set beautifully, with sunflowers and wildflowers at the center of the table. Their best china and wine glasses were properly placed. Their silverware was passed on by Beverly's grandparents.

Sofia and Yolanda asked the men and the kids to head to their chairs, while the ladies placed the assorted pies on a fold-up table for later.

The elders said a prayer before serving the food. Separately, the men were excited to eat, and the kids couldn't contain themselves because of their favorite meal—baked mac and cheese. Pies were always made from scratch by Beverly. She learned how to bake from her mom and grandma when she was ten.

Food was being passed around; everyone was really having a great time together.

After about an hour into the meal, Jonathan Sr. said that he was going to Skype Matthew and Jennifer because he had good news to share. Beverly was especially happy because the good news would benefit the family—much-needed news for his family. Beverly had one outstanding medical bill that was weighing a little bit on them financially.

Jonathan Sr. had set up a TV in the dining room, especially for Matthew and Jennifer, so they could see everyone together during their stay at the university.

He asked Matthew and Jennifer to join the call via Skype. It was planned by their dad, so Matty and Jen made time for this reason. Jonathan Sr. said, "I have some exciting and much-needed news for my family."

He couldn't contain his joy and nervously said, "Not only did I get the raise, I have also been promoted to be the new director of parks and recreation at the Grand Canyon National Park." Everyone jumped with gladness, and all hugged and congratulated Jonathan Sr.

You could see the relief on Beverly's face. She gave him a great, big kiss that lasted for about fifteen seconds. The family said, "Yuck! We don't want to see that." They all started laughing and then toasted for Jonathan Sr. Matthew and Jennifer were extremely happy for their mom, dad, and siblings. Jennifer, Beverly, the girls, and the rest of the ladies got a little emotional as they looked at each other. It was a tender moment.

Lastly, Genny ran to her father and said jokingly, "Now, where is my allowance?" Everyone laughed again at Genny's little antics. They kept on congregating for the rest of the evening. The men celebrated with cigars in the backyard.

They cleaned up everything and sat in the living room, talking, laughing, and dancing to their favorite tunes till the kids fell asleep on the shoulders of their grandparents. They took the kids to their rooms while the adults spent a little more time together.

Beverly took Jonathan Sr. aside and said, "It would be a good idea for my parents to spend the night because it was getting late." He agreed.

Her parents were happy to stay over. Beverly's parents were set up in the extra room and got settled in. They left some things the last time they stayed over, so it was convenient.

Beverly and Jonathan Sr. sat a little while in the living room after everyone had settled in. They discussed how the evening went and talked about the good news.

"It was a long time coming, honey," Beverly said.

Jonathan Sr. hugged his wife intensely, and she returned it threefold. She whispered in his ear, saying, "I love you so much after all these years. Without you, Jonathan, I would be lost."

Jonathan Sr. got a little emotional and said, "I love you even more today than on day one. Since we met, I laid my eyes on you." They stood in silence for a few minutes, looking adoringly at each other, and headed upstairs, hugging each other.

They lay down and fell asleep in each other's arms, smiling.

Chapter 3

Part 1
Kathy and Derrick's Reunion

After months of separation between Kathy and Derrick, they needed to catch up and talk about work, family, and their future.

Kathy was headstrong about joining Derrick in Williamsburg, Virginia. Derrick already knew it was going to be very hard to convince Kathy to move.

After they had a discussion prior to Derrick moving to Virginia, she said to Derrick, "Just let it be." They carried on with their conversation about life, work, and health.

So rather than talking about moving together to Virginia, they made plans to go out to eat dinner with their fathers, Charles and Victor, and Derrick's mom, Janet.

Each called them not to make any plans on Wednesday night. It was their turn to pay for a meal for a change. Kathy asked if she could invite her mom, Dedee, to join them. Charles hesitantly said, "I don't know. It's entirely up to you." He didn't resent Kathy's mom, Dedee, anymore, but he still had some doubts.

Kathy said, "Okay. I'll make some plans separately with Derrick and Dedee."

Charles was okay with it. He said to Kathy, "You are grown now, and you can spend time with your mom if you wish to do so."

Charles told Kathy that he had met a woman and wanted Kathy to meet her. Her name was Veronica Stevens. He said to Kathy that he spoke about her all the time to Veronica. He had been dating her secretly. He wanted to be sure about his relationship with Veronica. Charles said, "I am dying for you to meet Veronica."

Kathy said, "It's about time, Dad. You have been working and living alone for the past ten years. You deserve to be happy. You are my favorite man in the world, and I want to see you happy." He was pleased that Kathy was happy that he found someone.

Kathy would be the judge of that. She was overprotective of her dad after her mom skipped on him. She saw how sad and angry he was when Dedee ran with another man. So this new relationship should have good intentions.

He mentioned, "Veronica had been working as a senior care manager for the Social Services Department in North Country for the past twelve years. She told me that she has two adult children who live on their own."

Dominick and Ashley had recently been married a year apart. Kathy shook her head to the left, looked at her dad, and said, "Will I meet them?"

He said, "For sure, because I really like her, and I know you will too."

Kathy asked, "How long have you been dating Veronica secretly?

Her dad said, "For a few months."

She said, "Okay.

Kathy started taking some extra classes to become a registered nurse. Kathy hadn't seen her dad for a few months, conversing only through Zoom.

She found a two-bedroom apartment with another nurse around the campus, where they were both attending the same classes. Kathy was still working at Planned Parenthood as a nurse and taking classes twice a week to become a registered nurse.

Her dad already knew about her classes and was thrilled that his daughter was pursuing furthering her career.

They spoke for a little longer and made plans to get together a week before Mother's Day. He said that he, Derrick, and Victor planned to throw a surprise celebration for Mother's Day for Derrick's mom, Momma Josephine, Denise, and Kitty. Kathy made plans with her mom, Dedee, to have lunch on May 2. Her dad, Charles, Kathy, and his new girlfriend, Veronica Stevens, would meet the day before she returned to one of her classes that week of the fifth.

They mapped out the dates perfectly.

The next day, Kathy and her dad made plans to meet.

Part 2

Charles, Victor, Kathy, and Derrick's Mother's Day Celebration

Kathy planned a pre–Mother's Day brunch for the second of May with Dedee, their mom; Momma Josephine, who lost her husband, Cody, from liver disease when Charles was in his early twenties; Janet and her mom; Kitty, whose husband, James, was suffering from long COVID; and Victor's mom, Denise, who was now in her mideighties. Victor and Janet had known Kathy since his dad, Victor Sr., had passed away eight years earlier of natural causes.

Charles's parents, Manny and Catherine, died in a car crash. Charles and his sister, Francine, who now lives in Rochester, New York, survived the crash when they were kids.

Kathy, Momma Josephine, Kitty, and Janet gathered at a restaurant that served the best brunch in town. They mingled for a few hours, chatting. Josephine and Kitty had known each other since Charles, Victor, Janet, and Francine were teenagers.

Kitty loved Kathy like a granddaughter, just as Momma Josephine loved Derrick like a grandson. Kitty's daughter died during the second stage of her pregnancy. Kitty never tried to have another baby after the death of her baby, Jillian. Kitty had Janet.

So the ladies played catch-up, ate their brunch, and then had some cocktails to pass the time. Kathy didn't say anything in front of her mom, Dedee, Momma Josephine, Janet, or Kitty about the surprise Mother's Day celebration that Charles, Victor, and Derrick were planning to throw in their honors. Dedee, on the request of Charles, wasn't invited to the celebration.

Kathy was feeling a little bad, so she told Josephine, Janet, and Kitty to bring some gifts for Dedee for obvious reasons. Kathy didn't spill anything in front of her mom, Dedee, about the Mother's Day celebration.

Dedee suspiciously thought that they were planning something that she wouldn't be invited to because of Charles. She decided to take it with a grain of salt and enjoyed her pre–Mother's Day brunch.

Dedee moved toward Kathy and whispered, "I know what's going on here."

Kathy nervously giggled and said, "Mom, you know you and Dad don't get along after what you have done to him. Dad is moving on with a new woman in his life named Veronica Stevens and didn't want you to ruin anything." Dedee could be overdramatic, so she said whatever.

Dedee never heard of Veronica Stevens but went on enjoying her time with Kathy and the other ladies. Dedee opened her gifts and complimented the gifts she received.

They had the last drink. They chugged the glasses before leaving the restaurant, except Kathy and Dedee, who stayed behind for another fifteen minutes before leaving the restaurant too.

Dedee seemed happy spending time with her daughter. She told Kathy that she understood why and didn't go on discussing Kathy's dad. Kathy was glad her mom didn't make a scene in front of people while leaving after their brunch date. Other families stayed at the same place. She kissed her mom. Dedee hugged her and said, "I'll see you soon, baby girl." They then went to their cars.

Part 3

Ladies Brunch

On May 4, Charles, Kathy, and Veronica planned to eat at Denny's to introduce Kathy to Veronica. Charles was a little concerned about how Kathy would react in front of Veronica. Kathy was poised and kind when she finally met Veronica.

Again, Kathy was very protective of Charles. Dedee's running off with another man without provocation was devastating to Kathy. She eventually forgave her mom for her own sanity. She went toward the table, where Charles and Veronica were waiting for Kathy to arrive. Then Kathy walked in with a smile and waved in their direction. People at Denny's noticed Kathy because she was a beautiful woman with the deepest blue eyes and curvy, just like her biological grandmother, who died from a rare kidney disease. The guests at Denny's just looked and turned back to their meals. Kathy was stunning.

Kathy sat with her dad and Veronica. Charles introduced Kathy to Veronica, and they shook hands. Veronica was a hugger but didn't want to pressure Kathy or make her feel uncomfortable, so she waited.

Veronica seemed a little nervous about meeting Kathy. Charles had mentioned Kathy's mom running off with another man and didn't want to be compared to Kathy's mom.

They sat and talked a little before ordering their meals. After an hour of eating and talking about Kathy's new endeavor, Veronica went on to show photos of her kids, Dominick and Ashley, to Charles and Kathy. They were having a good time swapping stories, among other things.

While Veronica excused herself to go to the restroom, Charles asked Kathy about meeting Veronica. She said, "I see how happy you are when you are together, and I like her too. She's funny and pretty, and I see how she looks at you. It seems she's really into you, and I am thrilled for you, Dad."

But Kathy had one question. Her dad said, "Shoot.

"Why hasn't she shown photos of her kids to you till now?"

He said, "I prefer to wait till you and Veronica get together first before showing off her grown kids." They were around Kathy's age, so it didn't matter. She was pleased with his response and smiled.

Veronica arrived back from the restroom. She continued chatting with Charles and Kathy for the rest of their time together, eating lunch.

Charles told Kathy and Veronica about expanding and opening another auto parts shop. He was the owner of an auto parts shop. Charles made a huge contribution to the community and his business. Charles's auto business was thriving because of his outsourcing through social media, flyers, and customers sharing with their family and friends to build his clientele.

Kathy was beside herself, and Veronica was genuinely excited for them. Kathy gently grabbed Veronica's hand and said, "You made my dad the happiest man on Earth, and I want to thank you for that."

Veronica was lost for words and said, "I want to continue making your dad happy because I see how he treats you. I know he would eventually love and care for me just like he does with you, Kathy." Kathy agreed.

Veronica expressed deeply to Kathy that she would never get in between her and her dad. She told Kathy a phrase. "The way a man treats his own daughter in his life is a reflection of how he would treat his woman." Kathy knew that her dad picked a good woman because of the way they acted around each other in front of Kathy.

Kathy was stunned at how comfortable they were around each other—comfortable in their new relationship. Kathy turned to her dad and said, "I am so proud of you, and I love you so much." Charles was a little embarrassed and blushed right in front of both.

Kathy turned to Veronica and said, "Look at how my dad's blushing and shit." They laughed hysterically. People noticed and enjoyed looking at Charles blushing. Kathy and Veronica were happy about Charles's new adventure. He was planning to open a new spot that would take place in a year or so.

Things were looking up—Kathy's new pursuit, Charles new venture, and Charles new relationship with Veronica.

Then Veronica asked both, "Would you like to go to my home to have lunch or even dinner someday?" She mentioned that Dominick was graduating from LSU with a degree in microbiology in June. Dominick loved playing football and tennis. She was planning a congratulatory lunch for her son, Dominick.

She said, "Ashley is coming home during her summer break from NYU and will be spending some time with us as well. Hope you can come." She told Kathy that her kids may have more in common with her than being around older folks.

Kathy giggled and said, "That would be lovely. Dad, what do you think? He said that if you're okay with it, I am okay with it, too."

Veronica said, "Wonderful! I'll let Charles know the exact date."

Kathy said, "Okay."

After that, everything was going according to Charles's plan. Charles just wanted Kathy to like Veronica. Kathy did. After their lunch together, they exited Denny's.

Kathy hugged her dad. Kathy and Veronica hugged each other like they knew each other longer than just that day. Charles grinned like a little boy with a new toy.

Veronica told Kathy that it was a pleasure meeting her. Charles kissed his daughter on the cheek and left.

On the way back, Charles and Veronica made plans to go to a sports bar to have a couple of drinks. They didn't live very far from the bar, so they walked there after parking the car at Charles's place. Halfway there, they decided to turn around and stay in instead of spending some time together at a bar.

They settled in and had a drink, sitting in the living room. They were listening to some of their favorite country tunes by Reba McEntire, Toby Keith, and Garth Brooks. It took months before they were comfortable enough to go to each other's homes.

They hadn't been intimate because it was the beginning of a new relationship for both in years. They didn't want to spoil it so quickly, but their sexual desires were too intense. They both wanted to do it badly. Charles hadn't had sex in years and was tired of jerking off, and Veronica was tired of using a dildo. She wanted the real thing. So did Charles; the desire to be inside a woman was overwhelming. It had been a while.

He wanted to feel the warmth of the virginal wall of a woman. She wanted to ride a dick and feel it inside her. Charles was well-equipped, and she knew about it. She felt it on top of his jeans. It was transparent. It was thick, just the way she liked it.

Obviously, they wanted each other. He slowly lifted her summer dress and started rubbing on her clitoris. Veronica gasped a little. Charles went down to her nether region and started to lick her up like an ice cream cone. She held his head steady while he continued licking and tonguing her down there.

Charles took some pillows from the sofa and placed them in the center of the living room. They took their clothes off slowly, turned away from each other, and started 69ing. They both burst for the first time as a couple.

He waited for a second and penetrated Veronica once again after they burst. With that hard-rock penis, he went all in, caressing her thighs. Veronica desired it. He looked straight into Veronica's eyes for a few seconds, turned her around with his bulging twenty-two-inch biceps, and doggy-styled her—long and deep.

Veronica wanted to stare directly into his hazel eyes, so she wrestled Charles down, and she rode on that dick like he was the last man on earth.

It went on a couple of times more. They came at the same time, screaming and hollering each other's names. Charles whispered at Veronica quietly and said, "I think my next-door neighbor heard us because their bedroom light just turned on."

They went to Charles's bedroom for one more round. This time, he picked Veronica up from her waistline, placed her at the edge of the bed, spread her legs wide, and rammed it again. Veronica was double-jointed. Charles took a little longer to cum after three rounds of passionate sex. Charles embraced Veronica for a bit before showering together, then they fell asleep naked.

Chapter 4

Part 1
The Men Meeting at the Local Bar

It was six days before the big Mother's Day celebration for the women in their lives. Charles, Victor, and Derrick met at a local bar to discuss their Mother's Day plans for Josephine, Kitty, Janet, and Denise. Francine was invited, but she didn't know that Charles had a surprise for her too.

The men gathered at an empty table that a couple of patrons had just left. Victor asked the patrons who were coming back to sit at the table. One of the men replied, "No, it's all yours. We weren't returning.

They sat down and ordered some pitchers of beer and nuts. They chatted about where they were going to throw the celebration.

Charles and Derrick wanted to throw it at the National Park, while Victor wanted to throw it at Claremont Hall. They went back and forth, laughing about it. Victor said, "An outdoor celebration is nice, but in a hall, we can hire a Mother's Day planner to organize the event." The guys looked at each other and were very interested in the idea. They knew that the ladies in their lives would love it.

Derrick, who was the youngest in the group, agreed that it was a fantastic idea. The other men agreed as well. They toasted and said, "Women make it so complicated, and we planned the Mother's Day celebration in an hour."

Victor said, "My friend Josh's wife, Christina, is a party planner. I will ask Josh to talk to her about hiring her for the special event." Once the guys were done talking and planning, they left the bar.

Victor, Charles, and Derrick went the following day to rent the hall from 3:00 to 9:00 p.m. before Mother's Day.

They had five days left to plan and hire a caterer, which wasn't hard. They used the same catering services for some other events Charles and Victor had thrown, calling for the space that was available. They jumped into action before someone else rented the space.

Luckily, no one did. Lastly, they ordered alcohol, sodas, and bottled water at a warehouse in Flagstaff for the event. Everything was going perfectly, without any issues, like God made it happen for those wonderful women.

Charles, as a surprise, invited Francine, her children, and her domestic partner, Bobby, to come. Both had suffered terrible relationships with their male counterparts and decided to switch teams—lipstick les.

Charles loved Francine. Her life choice didn't matter to Charles. If Francine was happy, so was Charles. Josephine was happy for Francine. Josephine supported Francine's decision. She confined herself to Josephine when she came out five years ago. It was very hard for Francine to tell Charles at first, but he embraced it. He, Kathy, and Josephine were progay, prochoice, and prolife.

Francine moved to Rochester, New York, after college to start a job as a project manager at a nonprofit organization. That's where she met Bobby, who was the director of social services at the same place Francine worked in Rochester. They met and became friends.

They clicked almost immediately. It wasn't till they went out a couple of times that they started to develop feelings for each other and started dating a year later.

It was a day before the celebration. Charles, Victor, and Derrick went to check on Christina's progress in the hall. The guys were amazed at how beautiful it looked.

The tables were draped with silk tablecloths. In the center of the tables were bowls with tropical fish swimming. There were purple, pink, and rose-colored balloons being inflated by her crew. A table especially made for Josephine, Kitty, Janet, Francine, and Grandma Denise was inspiring.

The guys thanked Christina for the work she was doing for their moms, grandmother, and sister. Christina said, "No problem."

Victor asked Christina if Josh was at work. She said, "No, he's working from home today."

Victor responded, "I will give Josh a call."

So Victor stepped away for a moment to call Josh. Josh's cell phone rang. He picked up his cell, and it was Victor on the other line.

They talked for about five minutes before Victor asked if they wanted to attend the celebration.

Josh said, "For sure, me and Christina will be there." They had been very close friends for over twenty years. Josh worked with Janet and Victor's business with their foundation. Victor and Janet decided to change some of their gourmet items and flavors to accommodate the diverse community members in Flagstaff. Everyone loved their gourmet shop because of the positive energy that came from Victor and Janet.

They welcomed everyone who came to the shop. Josh was working with Charles, Victor, and Janet on their causes. Josh had done two tours overseas. The project was very close to his heart.

Josh prepared everything for his family, just in case he needed to return. POSSIBLY...

Victor finally gave a name to the project. Victor shared it with Janet and Josh before the community board approved the project. He had named it "USA Kids of Troubled Afghanistan," dedicated to the men and women serving overseas and parents who lost someone in Afghanistan (fictional story). It was for the children of Afghanistan who were born in the US and US citizens alike.

Victor and Janet had raised over $500,000 so far, not including the food, water, and personal hygiene products from the community. That also had a relative fighting a war that was taking countless lives in the process.

Victor stepped outside again to the hallway to call Josh, just to tell him, "Thank you, Josh. Your wife is doing a great job in the hall. Talk to you tomorrow," and he proceeded to go back inside.

Charles, Victor, and Derrick exchanged some details about the caterers and their staff serving the meals to make sure there were enough water bottles for the guests who didn't drink alcohol, a DJ, and possibly a live band from the bar, where the guys would frequently have drinks in the neighboring area of Flagstaff.

Charles called Francine to remind her about her flight leaving at 3:15 p.m. that day. Francine said, "I can't wait to see you, Kathy, Momma Josephine, and our friends."

Charles replied, "I can't wait to see you and my twin nephews, Barry and Billy, and Bobby.

The crew moved around as they were about to finish the final touches to the hall, as instructed by Christina. The guys were really pleased with how everything looked. They exited the hall and ordered lunch at a nearby hero shop. They ordered their favorite-style sandwiches, a hero, and a beverage before heading back to Claremont Hall.

When Victor, Charles, and Derrick went to check in to see if everything was completed, Christina's crew just finished. It was charming and flowy. Sure enough, it looked so beautiful. Just right for Momma Josephine, Kitty, Francine, Denise, and Janet.

The tables looked lovely; the main table was decorated with the things they liked. The flower arrangements around the ladies' table were stunning.

Orchids, roses, and wildflowers were so colorful. They just couldn't stop staring at the flower arrangements. It made the entire hall smell nice and relaxing. Charles checked if the air conditioner could stay on because of the flowers. The manager of the hall said, "Yes, it can."

They looked at each other, nodding their heads with approval, and clapped at Christina.

They chatted about how to send the money directly to her Zelle account to pay the remaining balance.

The men thanked her again. They told her that the ladies in their lives were going to be impressed and surprised.

Christina successfully finished the job on time. Victor said, "Did Josh call to tell you?"

She said, "Yes, like ten minutes after you guys left to the hero shop." She thanked the guys for inviting her and Josh to the celebration.

"Thanks again for choosing my services," Christina said. Christina received the $8,000 she asked for without any delay from Victor, Charles, and Derrick.

Victor said, "You should thank your husband."

Christina said, "I will, in a special way." The guy blushed like they knew Josh was going to get it—the "king for the night" treatment.

They all exited the hall at the same time, went to their cars, and waved goodbye.

That same afternoon, after visiting Claremont Hall, Charles and Kathy went to pick up Francine, Bobby, and the twins at the Flagstaff Pulliam Airport in separate SUVs.

They spun around the airport when they spotted them. They beeped their horns as they briefly parked to load their luggage into the two SUVs that fit at least six people comfortably in each one.

They all hugged everyone and got in because they saw people in their cars beeping their horns like maniacs.

Charles and Kathy were so sweet to see them. Momma Josephine knew they were coming to Flagstaff. The Mother's Day celebration was a secret that even Francine didn't know anything about.

Barry and Billy just turned four when their mom's messy divorce from Barry Sr. was finalized. It was finalized just before Francine was offered the job as a project manager in Rochester, New York.

Charles and Francine brought up stories when they were young. They both thanked Josephine and Cody for raising them as their own when their parents passed away in the car crash. Bobby listened intently, and the boys were on their minitablets.

The twins were asked to put their headpieces on because they were literally talking over each other over the noise on the tablets.

Barry and Billy were good boys and listened without any fuss. Barry and Billy were entertained by their tablets. As a matter of fact, it didn't matter to Barry and Billy; they were smart kids. When it came to adult conversation, they minded their own business.

The ride wasn't too far—about seventeen to twenty-four minutes away from Charles and Josephine's home. When everyone arrived at Momma Josephine's home, she embraced Francine, Bobby, and the twins. Josephine had just finished cooking for them. They conversed for a bit.

Josephine hadn't seen Francine, Barry, and Billy since they were four; now they were nine. The boys hadn't forgotten about Momma Josephine and Dada Cody.

After Cody passed, she got a little depressed. Her family meant everything to her. She cherished every moment with her family whenever they came to town.

Josephine had a brother, Johan, and a sister, Cindy, who remained in Minneapolis, Minnesota, with their children after she moved to Arizona with Dada Cody, Charles, and Francine.

Cody, Nathan, and Johan Jr. are still living at home. Johan's youngest son, Johan Jr. (twenty-two); an older daughter, Amanda (twenty-four); and Cindy's son, Cody Nathan (twenty). They worked and contributed at home while living there. No questions were asked.

Charles remembered that his aunt, uncle, and their kids still lived in Minnesota. They shared the holidays back and forth. It was a shame that they couldn't make it to the event. Charles said he planned to give a video copy of the event to Johan and Cindy.

Charles said that he would call them through Skype to video chat with the rest of the family during the celebration. Charles reminded Johan and Cindy during a three-way conversation that it was a surprise, so they should not say anything to Momma Josephine. They said, "Okay." Josephine was going to love this surprise. She always enjoyed surprises. Cindy said, "Yes, she does enjoy surprises."

Charles said in a kind manner, "Momma Josephine and Daddy Cody took good care of me and Francine our entire lives. She deserves that and more… Daddy Cody must be smiling in heaven." They agreed and finished up talking on the three-way.

Part 2
Mother's Day Celebration

Mother's Day arrived after all the planning, secrets, and gathering of their families and friends to come and celebrate Mother's Day with them.

Everything was going smoothly. The ladies were getting ready. Kathy was helping Momma Josephine with her hair and light makeup. Kitty and Janet were helping Grandma Denise get ready. Grandma Denise was going to wear a lovely long linen dress with a light sweater over it.

Josephine was wearing a salmon chiffon dress with a light sweater on top. Janet was wearing a strapless dress with a translucent strap that held the dress up and a blazer, while Kitty was going to wear a red dress that looked amazing on her.

The guys looked handsome in their suits. They made sure that the stretch limo arrived on time. The ladies thought that they were going to a fancy restaurant. They didn't know about the surprise that was coming their way—entirely different from what they thought it would be.

Once the limo arrived, the men blindfolded the women, so they didn't see where they were going. The ladies were saying, "Are you nuts? For what purpose?" Charles, Victor, and Derrick explained that it was for a good reason, and they wanted to surprise them.

They looked at each other and said, "Fine." Derrick, Victor, and Charles guided them into the stretch limo while blindfolded. Kathy was already in the limo at the request of her dad.

Kathy remained quiet while the ladies were blindfolded. You could see the joy on their faces. The ladies were going to be speechless about what they had done for them. Mother's Day was special. This surprise was bigger than life for Josephine, Janet, Kitty, Francine, and Grandma Denise. Kathy kept it to herself till the day of the event.

The men remained calm during the whole trip to Claremont Hall. The ladies were chatting and seemed super excited about celebrating as a group. It hadn't happened in a year to have dinner outside home.

All the ladies would only celebrate Mother's Day intimately with family and close friends. They couldn't even imagine what was about to transpire.

Everyone in the limo was ready to surprise the women in their lives, anxious to show them how much they loved them. Charles's mom, Josephine; Kathy's grandmother; her aunt, Francine; Victor's wife, Janet; Derrick's mom; Grandmother Kitty; and Derrick's Grandma Denise were going to have a ball. It was only a premonition in theory.

As they approached Claremont Hall, the men took the ladies by their hands, helped them out of the limo, and took them up the stairs before entering the hall. Kathy came out last and locked the door behind her.

The limo driver was paid for the day, so he just sat in the limo, talking to his wife and kids and playing some games. They were ready to have fun.

Charles, Victor, and Derrick continued taking their time, so they wouldn't slip or fall, and entered. The music was playing, and all the guests were sitting patiently till the guests of honor got there. The guests were whispering, so no one could hear them.

As the men were escorting the ladies into the dance hall, they could hear everyone getting up from their seats to yell surprise once the blindfolds were removed.

The men signaled with their hands to the guests. Saying, "Not yet" and to wait. Then the blindfolds came off, and everyone in the hall yelled, "SURPRISE!" The ladies got emotional and held their hands over their mouths with a surprised look that was priceless. Cameras flashing and hands clapping so loudly filled the room.

They couldn't stop looking at the guests. The ladies were amazed at how everything looked. The guests, the food, and the music were spectacular.

Everyone was having a great time dancing and eating. The ladies were so overwhelmed that the men in their lives would do something so grand for them.

They were talking among themselves about how they wanted to plan a Father's Day bash for the men. After overhearing Janet and the other ladies at the table chatting, Victor asked, "What are you scheming over there?"

They said, "Nothing," at the same time.

Janet said to Victor over the sound of the loud music, "This is a lady conversation. So PLEASE! Go with Derrick and mingle with the guests."

Victor replied with a neck back and perched lips, "Okay, I didn't mean to overhear your conversation." Victor looked toward the entrance of the door and saw Josh and Christina as they were walking in.

Christina and Josh had a bag of gifts for Janet, Josephine, Francine, Denise, and Kitty from their business and handed them over to Victor to place with the other gifts. There were at least one hundred gifts so far, and there were only sixty guests who arrived at the celebration.

Charles, Victor, Kathy, and Derrick invited one hundred guests. There were six cancellations because of some family matters that came up days before.

Even if there were sixty or one hundred guests, they were still having a great time. The ladies were having an awesome time at their party.

Charles called Kathy to let her know that he and Veronica were on their way. Kathy said, "Dad, I am glad you are bringing Veronica with you. I really didn't want you to come without Veronica. You both look great together. I like her very much. I see a great relationship afoot between you two. People started talking when you were going to find a woman. I already told a few people that you won't be alone any longer."

Charles said, "Honey, I really don't care what people say."

Kathy said, "I am proud of you. You have finally found someone like Veronica who makes you happy."

Charles said, "Yes, she does, honey. I have been thinking about that. I am relieved that you are okay with her coming."

She replied, "Of course, Dad. I am glad you are with her. Momma Josephine is waiting to meet Veronica."

Charles was nervous about introducing Veronica to Momma Josephine. Dedee destroyed Charles confidence in women and his happiness after leaving him in a lurch to raise Kathy on his own. She was relentless about him meeting the same kind of woman as Dedee.

Momma Josephine was surprised when she saw Charles walk in with Veronica in his arms, smiling at each other. Everyone turned in amazement at the fact that Charles looked happy with a new woman in his life.

No one could stop looking at Veronica. She was beautiful, with light-brown eyes and long silky black hair, and a body to die for. Some of the women were getting a little jealous of her, like school-girls at a prom.

The men were gagging at Veronica. The men were thinking about how Charles could find such a beautiful woman as Veronica. Don't forget Charles was handsome, and he could get any woman he wished.

As Kathy was passing, she heard the men talking about her dad and the new woman in his life. She turned to them as she was walking by and said, "My dad is a handsome man, and any woman would be a foul not to be with a man like him." The men shut up as quickly as they were gossiping.

Charles and Veronica were walking toward the table where Momma Josephine and the ladies were sitting. Momma Josephine was really surprised to see Charles with this lovely woman in his arms.

"Momma, can you come with me? I want to introduce you to this beautiful woman whom I really like, and I hope you will too," said Charles, as he gently took Momma Josephine by the hand and went to an empty table.

Kathy mentioned at the table that her dad had a surprise for Momma Josephine an hour earlier. Charles started a video call with his Uncle Johan, Aunt Cindy, and their kids via Skype to join them with the rest of the family.

Momma Josephine was beside herself. When she saw her brother, sister, and their kids, she started to weep. They wished their sister a happy Mother's Day, to have a lot of fun, and that they would be seeing her soon.

Momma Josephine looked at Veronica. Veronica felt nervous, but she had a way of making people feel comfortable around her. She worked with people every day, so Veronica had the knack of bringing people together to have fun.

So Veronica said, "It is a pleasure meeting you finally. Charles raved about you so much. Sorry, Charles kept it a secret till today."

Momma Josephine giggled immediately and said to Charles, "I am going to grab you by your ear for not introducing this lovely woman to me."

Such a good vibe from Veronica, Momma Josephine noticed it quickly. She said to Veronica, "I like you already," as they were conversing at the empty, reserved table.

As they sat down to talk, Momma Josephine turned to Veronica briefly and said, "Please take good care of my Charlie. I don't want him to get hurt again. Did he mention Kathy's mom?" Veronica was a little hesitant to say Momma Josephine so soon. Veronica called her Mrs. Villanueva.

Momma Josephine said to Veronica, "You can call me Momma Josephine any time. Charles looked stunned. Momma Josephina wasn't that receptive to any woman after Dedee. She was protective of Charles and Francine. She never wanted to see her children sad.

That's when Francine, Barry, Billy, and Bobby came behind Momma Josephine and kissed her head. Josephine was so happy that they were able to come. Francine and her family were there. Charles and Kathy were there. Johan, Cindy, Johan, and Cody Nathan were there. Even if it was on video, they were still there in spirit.

She embraced them. Francine and her family were introduced to Veronica. Francine said, "I hope we didn't interrupt your conversation."

Charles said, "Not at all. Come sit with us so you can get to know Veronica."

Charles said to his entire family that he'd been seeing Veronica for the past six months. He didn't want to spoil it to see where the relationship was going before telling anyone. Veronica agreed. They were all happy for Charles. They just wanted him to be happy and finally meet a woman who would love and care for him.

They were all into Veronica, like they had known her for years and years. Veronica felt like family, and she was a little touched by the way she was welcomed to the family so easily. It was all about the vibes.

Kathy joined her classmates who were invited to the celebration. One of Kathy's classmates was a mother of three children who was achieving her goal of becoming a registered nurse in pediatrics.

Kathy and Susan were taking a few classes together, so she invited Susan and a few other classmates to have a good time. The girls wanted to go to have fun, eat, and dance with single men at the celebration.

Kathy reminded her classmates, "Please don't embarrass me."

The girls laughed and said, "Kathy, we will never embarrass you. We like you too much to do that. We will conduct ourselves like respectable women."

Kathy said, "Have fun." Kathy went to accompany her family at the table.

It was thirty minutes before Josephine realized that Kitty and Janet were at the table alone, having a good time without her. She waved at the ladies, and the ladies waved back at Josephine and her family.

Kitty and Janet weren't worried because she was with her family. Family was everything, as was Janet with Victor, Derrick, and some family from the outer town who came in support of Kitty and Grandma Denise.

Everyone else was dancing, eating, and having a ball.

Charles took his mom and danced a little. Momma Josephine came from an era that enjoyed dancing and having fun. Especially when she and Cody were younger, they would go out with friends to dance halls and dance till their feet hurt.

The rest of the family joined. Veronica was asked by Francine and Bobby to join as well. She was honored and danced alongside Charles and her new extended family.

Kathy and Derrick danced a little. Janet, Kitty, and Victor joined in too. Grandma Denise looked at them, snapping her fingers and waving them side by side. Everyone gave them the floor and watched them dance like a family who just wanted to have a good time.

Charles left the dance floor, propping up the microphone at the DJ booth. He, Victor, Derrick, and Kathy had written a special letter to Momma Josephine, Kitty, Denise, Janet, and Francine.

As Charles was about to tell the DJ to lower the music a little, he summoned Victor, Kathy, and Derrick to come up to the stage to say a few words.

Victor went first because this was his suggestion to have it at Claremont Hall.

Victor investigated the crowd of friends and family who celebrated with them. Then he looked at the ladies who were being honored at the table, designed especially by Christina.

"We are here to thank you for all you have done for your family, from raising us to healing our boo-boos, to feeding and clothing us, and sending us off to school and then to college. There are words that cannot express how much you mean to us—to me, Charles, Kathy, Derrick, Francine, and our community. You made this possible so everyone can see how special you are as a mom and grandmother to us all."

The hall was roaring with claps and whistles. He made a sign of a heart and turned to the ladies and said, "We all love you."

The ladies experienced all sorts of emotions at that moment—crying, laughing, and then hugging each other.

They continued by saying that this day was for them because they were mothers every day. Charles, Kathy, Francine, and Derrick read a poem about moms and their struggles. Charles asked his sister, "Francine read one verse, and the rest followed."

It moved the room. Everyone was so attentive to the whole celebration that they talked about it for weeks. It left an impressionable mark on everyone who attended.

Before the guests started to leave, one by one and couple by couple, they went to the ladies to say their congratulations and started exiting the dance hall.

Josh and Christina went to the ladies last to say congratulations. Everyone at the table told Christina how lovely everything looked. Christina said, "I am glad you loved it." They nodded yes before they left.

Everyone was so nice to clean up the mess at their tables. It alleviated the stress of cleaning. People chipped in by stacking up the chairs. The patrons worked hard. Everyone gave handsome tips to the waiters, servers, and DJ, who made everything go smoothly.

By 9:15 p.m., Charles and Victor, with their families, had closed the hall. They hopped on the limo to take them home.

Derrick and Kathy decided to catch up with what had been going on with their future. When they got out of the limo, Derrick wanted to speak to Kathy as she went inside.

Kathy said, "Not this again."

Derrick said, "Yes, this again. We have been separated for months now, and I can't spend another day without you. We have been through everything together since we were kids. Our parents practically put us together. How much longer will it take for us to start our lives? We talked about having kids and living in a modest home. We planned to be together for life. What changed?"

Kathy stood quietly and said, "Derrick, you know I love you, and I have cared for you since the first day we met. We were on the same bus heading to school when we locked eyes, but this moving away scares me. Moving away from my family and your family kills me."

Derrick assured Kathy that everything would be set up for her if she made up her mind to go. "I will wait for you when you finish your studies to become a supervising registered nurse. Let me know where we stand."

Kathy assured Derrick that she had been faithful and would continue to be faithful to him. He replied with the same sentiment about being faithful and loyal to Kathy.

Derrick asked Kathy to have dinner with him in a couple of days before he went back to Virginia. She said, "Okay, I would love to go out to dinner with you."

They looked at each other, kissed, and embraced each other without forgetting to grab each other's asses before breaking apart from one another.

Kathy and Derrick said to each other, "See you later, babe." They ended the night with another kiss. He watched her go inside, and he headed to his parents' home.

Chapter 5

Part 1

Beverly's MRI Appointment and Blood Work

Three and a half weeks had passed, and Beverly was anxious about her MRI and blood work results from Dr. P. Kingston. Beverly was a little scared, but she didn't worry about the results. Jonathan Sr. and Mrs. Daniel went with her to her appointment for moral support.

Jonathan Sr. would start his new director of parks and recreation position in a couple of days, so he asked for two days off to support his wife. Jonathan Sr. asked his supervisor to see if the request was approved. Miguel approved the request.

Jonathan Sr., Beverly, and Mrs. Daniel planned to meet at Dr. Kenley's office, then went to eat lunch at the Descanti-Cartwright home before picking up Tammy, Jonathan Jr., and the always funny little Miss Genny.

Beverly was somewhere else with her thoughts. Jonathan Sr. and Mrs. Daniel noticed almost immediately that Beverly was in her own mind about the MRI appointment.

Jonathan Sr. said to Beverly, "Baby, are you okay?"

"Just thinking about you, my beautiful children, and Mrs. Daniels. You know, whatever happens, you are the first to know about it," said Beverly.

Mrs. Daniel didn't want to interrupt the moment between Jonathan Sr. and Beverly, but Beverly did ask Mrs. Daniel for words of wisdom because of her experience with breast cancer in the '80s.

Mrs. Daniels said, "First, I totally understand the fears that come with a cancer diagnosis. With modern medical technology and treatment on the rise, you have a better survival rate than I had in the '80s. Look at me now. I have been in remission for twenty-five years after my second diagnosis.

Beverly looked more relaxed after Mrs. Daniels revealed her diagnosis in more detail. It helped Beverly get it out of her head and focus on what she was going to do if the cancer came back or continue to move forward on her remission next stage. "I will be here to support you for whatever you need, Beverly," Mrs. Daniels said.

Jonathan Sr. was thrilled. Beverly would be okay with the support and love from her family. He was surprised to hear about Mrs. Daniels revealing her experience with breast cancer and her recovery.

The day had come. They all went to Beverly's appointment with Prisilla. They were all holding hands, like any family would in this situation. They sat down and waited.

When Prisilla came out of her office, Jonathan Sr. asked if he and Mrs. Daniels could stay if they liked to be with Beverly to hear her results. Prisilla said, "Let me get a HIPPA form for you and Mrs. Daniel to sign before letting you come with Beverly." They agreed and signed the HIPPA form.

Dr. Kingston escorted them to her office and asked them to have a seat. Dr. Kingston looked and said, "Beverly, don't worry about your results." Beverly closed her eyes and took a deep breath. So did Jonathan Sr. and Mrs. Daniel.

Dr. Kingston rested her hand on Beverly's forearm and said, "All your tests and blood work all came back negative. All the lymph nodes and cancer cells from your MRI on both breasts have shrunk dramatically.

Beverly decided to ask Dr. Prisilla Kingston a couple of questions privately with Jonathan Sr. next to her. She asked Mrs. Daniels to step out of the office for a moment. She needed to ask some personal questions. Mrs. Daniels agreed and stepped out to the reception area and waited till they came out of Dr. Kingston's office.

She asked Prisilla, "Can I make love to my darling husband?" Jonathan Sr. and Prisilla looked at Beverly like it was a fair question to ask.

Dr. Kingston said, "Yes, you can."

Beverly asked the second question to Prisilla, "Can a woman be diagnosed with vaginal stenosis after chemo or radiation?" Prisilla looked flabbergasted that Beverly knew about vaginal stenosis. In Prisilla's mind, she must've read it somewhere by searching on Google.

Prisilla told Beverly that the only way it could be determined was to have a vaginal or pelvic exam by a gynecologist.

Dr. Kingston said, "If you like, I can schedule an appointment with a gynecologist friend of mine. Dr. Alvarado will examine you and see if you are suffering from vaginal stenosis after chemo."

Beverly said, "Yes, because I read that it can narrow the vaginal wall, and it can be extremely uncomfortable to penetrate deep inside the vagina." Dr. Kingston scheduled the GYN appointment for Beverly with Dr. Alvarado.

Prisilla said, "Keep in mind that it doesn't happen to every woman. If you feel more comfortable finding out if you are suffering from VS, I can set up an appointment for the seventeenth at 11.20 a.m. with Dr. Alvarado.

Jonathan Sr. was taken back by the questions she asked Prisilla. He just stood there, listening. He said, "Should I step out?"

Beverly said, "No, honey. I want you here with me."

Jonathan Sr. contained himself while hearing the results. What he heard from his wife's mouth excited him. He got up and hugged his wife after Prisilla made one of the happiest days come true for his family.

Beverly just stood there, shocked; her doubt and fear were immediately washed away. Prisilla mentioned to Beverly that she would continue monitoring her recovery in the later months of Beverly's care. "Continue taking your treatment as prescribed. I will set up another appointment in three to four months."

Beverly was so happy that her appointment with Prisilla would be three to four months after attending her appointments every other week. Beverly was doing well with her medications. In her mind, it was a step toward the right direction.

Mrs. Daniel congratulated Beverly. Jonathan Sr., in his heart, won't lose his wife to cancer. She was the most precious commodity God ever created.

They had lunch at one of their favorite places to eat. They talked for about an hour before picking up the kids from school.

Jonathan Sr. and Beverly planned to speak via Skype to Matthew and Jennifer in a week to process the news about their mom's progress. Tammy, Jonathan Jr., and Genny didn't understand their mom's condition, but they were willing to share the news with them.

It must sink in first before sharing.

They continued to live their lives as normally as possible till Beverly shared the news.

A week had flown by, and Beverly was ready to call Matthew and Jennifer via Skype. The day before Jonathan Sr. started his new position at the National Park, Beverly made it happen.

The kids were let out early from school at their parents' request. Their teachers understood that it was important news to share with their family.

So once the kids were home from school, Bev called her elder children. Matthew and Jennifer were waiting to hear from their mom. They were both optimistic and positive to finally hear the news they had been waiting for.

Then came the news. "My babies, I am going to be fine. My results were fantastic. No recurrence of cancer. I have a follow-up appointment in three months from today."

The kids were so happy for their mom that they pretended to hug her. The kids were doing the same. Genny said cleverly, "Matthew and Jennifer, how are you doing that?" They all started to crack up. It seemed that little Genny knew what to say when she wanted her family to laugh. It was comforting.

Matthew and Jennifer told everyone that they had to return to their classes. Their mom and dad said, "Talk to you soon."

After talking to the kids on Skype, Mrs. Daniels made a light snack for Tammy, Jonathan Jr., and Genny before dinner. Jonathan Sr. went to their bedroom to rest before dinner.

After Beverly had rested, Mrs. Daniel prepared lunch for the kids for school. Mrs. Daniel prepared dinner before she left for the day.

Part 2

Dr. Prisilla Kingston's New Love Interest

Prisilla was on her way to shop for some groceries for her dad, Kevin, while he's at work. She bumped into Jeremy from the conference in Thailand. He was there, but for a different kind of medical conference at the hotel.

Jeremy was tall, mocha-skinned, and had broad shoulders that Prisilla found creamy to eat. He had nice light-brown eyes that could attract any woman who came his way. His curly jet-black hair looked silky in the sunlight.

They greeted each other. "What are you doing here in Flagstaff, Arizona?" Then they embraced one another.

She thought, *Damn, he smells delicious.*

In his mind, he wanted to take her in the car to do things that he hadn't done with a woman in a long time. Jeremy had been abstinent from sex, and Prisilla hadn't been with a man in a while because of her work.

They accompanied each other to the giant supermarket that you can get lost in. Looking at the different types of food choices, healthy drinks, and more was just what the doctor ordered, especially for Jeremy and Prisilla.

They had seen each other several times on different medical conference trips, like in Milan, London, and the Asian Coast. They caught each other's eyes during and after the conferences they attended but never reacted to their desires.

It was an instant attraction. Finally, they could talk outside the medical conferences face-to-face. Bumping into one another at the parking lot in the supermarket brought some sexual tension between them.

Again, Prisilla asked Jeremy, "What are you doing here?"

Jeremy answered, "My grandparents, Betty and Carlson, who raised me, live in Flagstaff. I am planning to move from Chicago to Flagstaff in a few months. I bought a home next to my grandparents."

He said he just needed to finalize the payments for his new home. He was being transferred to the hospital in Flagstaff, and then he would move his property to his new home.

She extended her congratulations. Now, Prisilla was happier that Jeremy would be living in Flagstaff—easy access.

Prisilla didn't want to give Jeremy the impression that she was eager. Prisilla, with eyes wide open, said, "That is fantastic."

Jeremy said, "I hope to see you more often when I move here to Flagstaff." She said yes and paid more attention to Jeremy, reading between the lines.

Jeremy was a little shy to ask. Asking Prisilla to go on a date was a small step for him. He was looking at the bigger picture. "Prisilla?" Jeremy politely asked. "Will you like to have dinner with me before I go back to Chicago?" She hesitated for a few seconds but gave him a thumbs up on the date.

Jeremy added, "Is that a 'yes'?"

She replied, "Yes, it's a date." Jeremy didn't care. All he was interested in was a long-term relationship with Prisilla. Quietly, Prisilla was thinking the same thing.

Jeremy and Prisilla continued chatting while shopping.

Both were in good shape. Both worked out. They bought practically the same things. She bought some food that her dad, Tim, requested.

They headed to their cars and exchanged numbers to set up a time and day to reach out to each other over the phone. Jeremy helped Prisilla load her groceries into her car.

Jeremy went to give her a hug and a peck on the cheek. Instead, they both gave each other a passionate kiss and then a hug. They didn't care if people saw them kissing. They both smiled after the kiss.

Jeremy held her hand like a gentleman did and guided her inside Prisilla's car. He bowed down at Prisilla like a knight for his queen.

Prisilla said, "Call me with the location, time, and day."

Jeremy said, "Expect my call." He didn't want to sound eager, so he asked, "What will be the right time for me to call you?"

She said, "Around 10:00 p.m. That's when my dad is resting for the day after work."

She mentioned that her dad, herself, her cousin Samantha, and her uncle Kevin worked at their private office, which they invested in together.

Jeremy said, "Wow! A family business, huh?"

Prisilla nodded and said, "Yes, we decided to invest in private practice outside the main hospital."

He said, "Prisilla, that is impressive.

Prisilla replied, "Yeah, we are doing well with our private clinic."

Jeremy almost forgot to mention that he had been offered a position as the director of pediatrics. He came from a family of highly decorated doctors, nurses, and caretakers for more than seven decades in Chicago, Illinois. He came from a strong and well-groomed family—classy and refined.

Jeremy went on to say, "My grandparents go to sleep around the same time too."

Prisilla exited the parking lot first; Jeremy placed his things in the back seat of this car and left the parking lot with a smile, listening to his favorite tunes—R and B.

Prisilla was thrilled to bump into Jeremy. She had had a crush on him since the first time she saw him in the lobby, checking in at the hotel in Milan.

Jeremy was deep in thought, thinking about Prisilla after bumping into her. *Is this meant to be?*

They were in a daze, thinking about the date.

Hypothetically speaking (a side-by-side image of them thinking at the same time about the same thing).

The feeling was so strong that you could feel the desire between them. Seeing each other once again was like a bolt of lightning that struck their hearts.

That same evening, Jeremy called Prisilla to set up a date to have a meal together. But Jeremy had other plans for Prisilla.

During the conversation, Jeremy told Prisilla in a deep voice, "Prisilla, can we plan something else than going to a stale fancy restaurant?" Prisilla was curious to know what kind of plans Jeremy was suggesting. She was down to do anything instead of going out. It would be more intimate, so they could focus on one another.

Jeremy wanted to plan a more intimate night at home—preparing dinner, having a few glasses of Italian Moscato, and some light music. Prisilla was exhausted from her day with her dad, doing laundry, writing clinical notes, making and rescheduling appointments on her computer, and making a meal for her dad, Tim, who was suddenly not feeling well.

Prisilla explained to Jeremy about her day—how exhausted she was and didn't want to be rude. She asked if it was okay to plan it for another day when she had free time. Jeremy understood. He asked if it was okay to talk more over the weekend before his return to Chicago. She said that it would be best to reschedule so there would be no interruptions or obstacles. Jeremy was impressed by her response. Jeremy said there was no problem.

To be precise, it would be better to plan it well in advance. He was pleased with the thought of planning it for another time, like when he returned to Arizona.

That weekend, Prisilla was off to catch up the following day over the phone with someone. She could see herself with Jeremy in the future. Jeremy seemed flexible with the idea of following up with Prisilla.

Jeremy told Prisilla that he wanted to see a movie to spend quality time with his grandparents, Betty and Carlson, and then have lunch with them.

She said, "That sounds good, Jeremy. I see you care a great deal about them!" His reply was absolutely.

They talked for about twenty minutes.

There were some sexual undertones in the conversation. They were thinking about how they were going to tear their clothes off and do unspeakable things to each other.

They talked about the last time they had any intimacy with the opposite sex. Again, they were thinking about the unspeakable things they wanted to do to each other. He was a sexual freak who enjoyed role playing, and she was a sexual being only with a man she's into. Jeremy mentioned to Prisilla that he was getting aroused by the conversation. She told Jeremy that she was getting a little wet from the sound of his voice.

Their intentions were in high gear. They were going to finally say to one another, "So many ways to fuck in every room in a home. But who's home?"

Their minds were racing after that conversation.

They both agreed to stop talking about it and agreed to call the next day.

Part 3

Samantha and Jacob's Baby News

Samantha and her fiancé, Jacob, sat down during a doctor's visit to get confirmation if they were expecting or not.

Dr. Alvarado, a gynecologist who would be seeing Beverly on a different day, asked them to enter his office to give them the good news. They were expecting a boy.

Now getting their families together to announce that a baby was on the horizon was going to be a little difficult.

They wanted to be sure they were expecting, so they kept it a secret for four months. Jacob's mom, Katherine, and his dad, Sean Garrisons, were Christians.

They believed that since they were only engaged, they shouldn't have children till they got married.

Both Jacob and Samantha's family knew that they had been engaged for two years now and planned to get married soon after. So sharing with her family would be easier.

Her dad, Kevin, was eager for her to have a baby to carry on Kingston's name.

Jacob's family liked Samantha a lot and found her perfect for Jacob. She was sweet, kind, and came from a long line of oncologists. She came from a good family too.

For Samantha's dad, Kevin, it would be his first grandchild. He always dreamed of having a grandchild with Samantha and Jacob one day. There were days that her dad struggled with remembering things because he was diagnosed with onset dementia.

Jacob and Samantha decided to share it with only a few people they trusted. Prisilla was one plus two more people who would keep it a secret till they planned the whole reveal party.

Jacob and Samantha did not tell anyone about the sex of the baby till the reveal, only Prisilla. Samantha and her fiancé, Jacob, decided to plan a surprise reveal party. Planning it in a perfect and decadent way and gathering their families and close friends was a fantastic way to share the news.

But first, he and Samantha needed to sit down with his parents to discuss their announcement, but only during the party they were throwing in July.

In their minds, they had already made the decision whether to tell them or not. Jacob's parents would have to adjust to the news. It would be their first grandchild too, and, in his heart, he knew they would be happy for them, regardless of their beliefs.

In two months, the surprise reveal party was on…

Samantha called her cousins, Prisilla (forty), Gigi (twenty), and Bernard (nineteen and a half), individually over the phone to tell them that she and Jacob were expecting a baby, but they should not tell anyone. Both said, "It will be perfect timing for us. We will be staying with our family during our summer break from college."

They could keep it a secret. As young kids, they would cover for one another even if it got them into trouble. Taking their privileges away was better than rating out each other.

Jacob told his aunt Vicky and her kids Philip, Leann, and Larry over the phone about the upcoming party in two months, but they should not tell his parents anything till then.

Aunt Vicky said, "Don't worry. I got you. Between me and you, I know it is good news about you and Samantha. I can feel it."

He said, "Thank you, Auntie."

Vicky was the sister of Catherine, Jacob's mom. Auntie Vicky was cool and down to earth. She raised her kids as a single parent, without their father in the picture, after being murdered by a rival who was charged with Philip Sr.'s death.

After her husband's murder was solved, Vicky and her kids would inherit property and a large sum of money from Philip Sr.'s successful business in antiques. She didn't know anything till an attorney called her to tell her that her husband had secretly given everything to her, Philip, Leann, and Larry and nothing to his family.

Jacob asked Vicky if she could be there with her kids and not make any plans for July 4. "It will be an indoor event. Me and Samantha will be planning everything. As soon as I find a perfect location, I will let you know, Auntie Vicky," said Jacob.

She said, "Okay. Count me in."

Vicky took up modern dancing in high school and in college, so dancing was in her blood.

First, they needed to find a reveal party planner to set up the way they had planned it in the heads—elegant but simple. It should not look overdone or understated but be subtle enough to shock people with excitement. They had their minds set on Victor and Janet's gourmet shop to do the catering. At least fifty people would be invited.

They would make sure that both their parents and the rest of their families were there by hook or by crook. Samantha told Jacob that her cousins would be there, for sure. Jacob told Samantha that his aunt and cousins would be there for sure too.

Both invited Samantha's sorority sisters and best friends. Jacob invited his frat boys. They remained good friends after college. They were the last in the group of friends who had a child or two already. Being in their late twenties, having a baby was part of their vision board. They all accepted the invitation for July 4. So far, there were twenty-nine guests on the list who said yes. Twenty-nine people who were invited to the reveal party would be mailed.

Now it would be time to get the rest of the family to come. They were confident that they would come. Samantha was starting to show, and people were noticing that she was pregnant.

Two days later, Samantha told her dad, Kevin, that they were expecting. He was overjoyed because his dream had come true. Then came Jacob to tell his parents, Catherine and Sean, that they were expecting. Jacob didn't want to reveal anything. Catherine would know; she was a mom. Sam couldn't hide anymore. She was showing.

Jacob was very concerned about the way they would react. Samantha, on the other hand, was expecting criticism from them. So Jacob and Samantha trotted over to his parents' home the following day and told them that they were expecting.

It was the contrary. Catherine would've been shocked at first. She changed her tune when she found out that they were expecting a baby, but Sean was a different story. He was disappointed, and he left the room for a moment. Then he came back and hugged them both. He started to show his manliness. He never liked to share his emotions. He felt people would view him as a weak man. This was his son. Eventually, he expected Jacob to carry on his name and legacy.

His one and only son—Jacob—was going to have a child with Samantha, whom they adored unconditionally. It was welcome news. She had a way of making things sound more positive than focusing on the negative. Catherine loved that about Samantha. Her sweet disposition and the way she looked at them with admiration were well respected.

Catherine and Sean asked about the sex. They stood firmly together and said, "You will find out at the reveal party on July 4. They loved that idea. "That was fair because if Samantha's dad didn't know the sex, why should we? No one should know," said Sean.

Part 4

Kevin's Neurologist Emergency Appointment

One day, during a visit between Kevin, Samantha, and Jacob, they were sitting and conversing in the kitchen. They were about to discuss the plans for the reveal party.

Out of nowhere, Kevin got so irate that he asked them to leave. Kevin told them that he didn't know who they were and started screaming and throwing things.

Samantha was so distraught over her dad that she immediately called her uncle, Tim, and her cousin, Prisilla, to come over as fast as they could because her dad was throwing things around the house.

Samantha told her cousin and uncle that she would explain a little more about what had happened when they arrived at her dad's home.

Tim and Prisilla asked the front desk receptionist to hold all new appointments and reschedule all upcoming appointments after taking care of a sudden family emergency.

Brenda said, "Okay, Dr. Kingston," referring to Tim. Brenda asked if she should leave early after rescheduling.

They both said, "Absolutely," and exited their private clinic to attend to Kevin.

They both knew this would happen eventually, so they were prepared to simmer down the confusion at Kevin's home with the techniques that Dr. Benning, the neurologist, provided in case of an emergency like this.

When they got there, they saw Kevin holding a pen in his hand. Sam and Jacob didn't know what to do in a situation like this. So Samantha and Jacob watched Tim and Prisilla use these techniques to help her dad relax and calm down.

Calmly, Tim was able to talk to his brother. Tim was also able to remove the pen from Kevin to prevent any harm to himself or anyone else.

Samantha and Jacob felt so helpless and held each other's hands for comfort and security. Samantha and Jacob went to the kitchen to talk again. Jacob was worried if this was going to affect Samantha and the baby. Samantha was shaking nervously. He supported his fiancée, Samantha, like he always did, to make her feel secure. She told Jacob that this was the first time she had ever experienced something like this with her dad since his diagnosis. She was sure that her dad would be okay with pessimism.

Prisilla called and paged Dr. Benning to schedule an emergency visit with him. He answered and agreed to see Kevin immediately after he was calm and relaxed.

So once Kevin was relaxed, they all got in the car and headed to see Dr. Benning. They were all a little scared, but the feeling wasn't permanent. It was just a feeling. Samantha and Jacob wanted to make sure that her dad would be okay, even if she thought he would or wouldn't be.

Dr. Benning was one of the most qualified neurologists in town and would take good care of Kevin quickly. Dr. Benning was declared to be a savant in his field.

After spending most of the day visiting Dr. Benning at the main hospital, Dr. Benning gathered the family together to give a more comprehensive take on Kevin's condition.

They were holding each other very closely and taking a deep breath. Dr. Benning told the family that they found an anomaly in his MRI and planned to admit Kevin for observation for a couple of days in the hospital.

Jacob sat down to get a grip, while Tim, Prisilla, and Samantha stood strong together as they always did. Jacob looked concerned but knew that Samantha's family got this. Jacob was able to alleviate any negative feelings that might consume him.

Dr. Benning mentioned to Kevin's immediate family that Kevin's medications would be adjusted to accommodate his medical needs. They would monitor his progress and inform them every step of the way.

The Kingston family was relieved but nervously optimistic. Kevin would be fine under the care of Dr. Benning and his medical team at the hospital.

They all waited till Kevin was placed in a room for observation. Once he was settled in, they were able to see Kevin. Kevin looked up at his family and said, "What the heck am I doing here?" Samantha, Tim, and Prisilla took turns explaining everything that happened at his home.

He said, "All I remember was that my baby, Samantha, and my future son-in-law, Jacob, were with me." Samantha stepped in and explained that she and Jacob were visiting him to start making plans for the reveal party in July.

"What reveal party?" Prisilla said, pretending not to know.

Samantha said, "Not now." She took a breather, then trailed carefully not to trigger her dad. Samantha didn't say too much about him, forgetting who they were.

Tim and Prisilla spoke to Dr. Benning about coming to visit Kevin more frequently at home after what happened to him. Dr. Benning didn't want to judge them, so he said, "Absolutely. Kevin needs attention."

Tim and Prisilla worked a lot at the clinic as well as the main hospital, so their time was spared. They were going to make it their business to spend more time with Kevin. Samantha worked with her family at the clinic and requested that she take some time off to focus on her health and her unborn child.

Kevin was speechless about the whole idea. Kevin looked around, embarrassed. They all supported him with love and understanding. For Kevin, that alone made matters more comforting for all of them.

That was when Dr. Benning and his team came to the room to see Kevin after speaking with Tim and Prisilla outside the room. He explained the steps they were going to take to improve his stability and make adjustments to his medications. Hiring a skilled registered nurse who has experience taking care of patients with dementia would be ideal.

The Kingston family agreed on what Dr. Benning was saying related to Kevin's mental health. Kevin became dismissive. He said all he needed was the love and support of his family. He didn't need any intervention or interruptions in his life.

Dr. Benning and his team assured Kevin that his life would not be interrupted. "You could continue living your life in comfort, dignity, and respect. We, doctors, look out for our people, and Kevin, you are our people."

Tim and Prisilla took Dr. Benning along with Samantha to discuss his treatment. Dr. Benning reiterated that Kevin's medication would be administered at a lower dose and to consider hiring a certified registered nurse to visit Kevin at least four times a week through VNS for the next four weeks. Just to make sure that Kevin understood everything that was happening, Dr. Benning repeated it again, so everyone was on the same page.

He added, "Kevin needs to be more stable mentally with the help of a skilled nurse. Prevention will be the best option for Kevin to avoid experiencing another episode like the one he experienced at home. It is important to have someone visit Kevin to help him around his home as well as to ease some of the load on the family."

They were all happy with the news, with Kevin in mind—Samantha and Jacob especially. They were hoping that her dad would be well enough to attend the most important day of Jacob and Samantha's lives.

After receiving the good news from Dr. Alvarado, it was extremely important for her dad to be there in person.

Kevin asked Samantha to come over to him. She went over to her dad. He reached out and rubbed her stomach. It was like he knew that his daughter and Jacob were expecting.

Kevin remembered that part. Sam was happy that he did remember.

Kevin was loved by everyone in his life. Family and close friends were flowing in with flowers, balloons, and baskets of assorted fruits. He wasn't on a strict diet, but after this situation, Dr. Benning told Samantha that Kevin would need to see a nutritionist to help Kevin make better choices in his eating habits and introduce more fish, fruits, and vegetables into his diet.

Prisilla and Tim agreed that Kevin should eat better.

They all said Kevin should eat better. Kevin brushed it off, but they were serious. It was a known fact among qualified nutritionists to say that eating dark greens could improve your memory.

Dr. Benning put Kevin on a no-red-meat, no-fatty-food diet. They all praised Dr. Benning for his recommendations on behalf of Kevin. It was great news to their ears.

Dr. Benning was one special individual. He showed he cared; he's responsible, and he has a "no play attitude for his patients."

Before the team exited the room, Dr. Benning told the Kingston family that he would keep them informed on any new developments during Kevin's stay at the hospital.

Prisilla took Samantha aside to talk about how they were going to share the responsibility during his recovery. Tim remained talking with Dr. Benning. Dr. Benning told Tim that there were new treatments coming. He would keep Kevin and the other patients in mind. Dr. Benning explained further that this new treatment would slow down the process of deterioration in the brain.

Tim asked curiously, "Are you planning to administer this new treatment to my brother?"

Benning said, "Only if nothing else works for Kevin. I am not considering it at this point till further testing." Tim seemed okay in finding better treatment for his brother, if necessary.

Tim related the same information to Samantha, Prisilla, and Jacob. He finished up with Dr. Benning and spoke to Kevin for about another thirty minutes.

The Kingston family, including Jacob, said to Kevin, "See you later," and exited the room. He looked at Kevin while they waited for the elevator. Kevin smiled, gave a thumbs-up to his family, and saw them disappear into the elevator.

Two days later, Kevin was discharged and waited for Tim to pick him up from the hospital. Prisilla and Samantha stood behind to set up things at home for her dad, Kevin.

The new CRN, Judy Velez, was interviewed by the Kingston family the day before Kevin returned home. The CRN provided paperwork that included her schedule. Once everything was set, CRN Judy Velez started working with Kevin the following day.

CRN Velez came from a family of nurses and phlebotomists for over fifty-five years combined. So everyone was absolutely smitten with CRN Velez because of her family history in the medical field.

Mrs. Velez had two girls, Jessica and Ally. Her husband, Tommy, of fifteen years, worked as an engineer before they met and then got married before having their daughters.

Kevin arrived home with Tim. They saw Prisilla, Sam, and CRN Judy Velez sitting in the formal room, waiting for them to arrive so they could talk about Kevin and his recovery.

The Kingston family enjoyed talking with CRN and asked if she would like something to drink (e.g., a bottle of water). She said, "Thank you, but I have one in my bag."

Kevin just sat there listening to the CRN's point-of-care services with his daughter, brother, and niece.

After a couple of hours, they were all impressed with CRN Judy Velez's seventeen years of experience in nursing. Samantha stood behind to give CRN Judy Velez a tour of the kitchen, bathrooms, and Kevin's bedroom.

Sam asked if she had a license to drive because she couldn't assume that she didn't drive. CRN Judy replied, "Yes, I do. I would be accompanying Kevin to his upcoming appointment with Dr. Benning in three weeks."

Samantha said, "We will be helping as well. My dad is my life, and I need to be a part of his recovery."

CRN said, "Of course. It would be beneficial for your dad to see his family involved to improve his state of mind and his health. Being present is essential for all patients' and clients' recovery." Sam was even more impressed with CRN Judy Velez and her skills.

Kevin, as well as Samantha, asked what she should be called. CRN asked everyone to call her Judy because it was about familiarity for the patient. "You want Kevin to feel comfortable in his own home," she said.

The Kingston family was truly overwhelmed by Mrs. Judy. Her idea of quality of life, as well as a point of care for patients, was impeccable. Prisilla said, "Where have you been?" jokingly. They had to laugh because they were thinking the same thing—Tim and Prisilla.

The Kingston family was glad that everything would go smoothly after speaking with Judy. Tim and Prisilla said goodbye to Kevin, Sam, and Judy.

Samantha and Judy spent the rest of the day with Kevin. Making smoothies once a day for Kevin with kale, Spanish cabbage, blueberries, strawberries, and apples, and daily lefty green salad, and preparing lean chicken without the skin for the next day.

Sam and Judy spoke to her dad about taking walks and exercising lightly. He liked the idea and was willing to try it.

Since Samantha still lived with her dad, she now knew what to do in case of an emergency with the instructions that Dr. Benning provided her to read.

CRN sat with Kevin, playing a couple of games of scrabble to sharpen Kevin's mind and skills. He loved to play scrabble, trivia pursuit, and clue. CRN Velez knew that word games helped the mind stay focused.

Judy started to put her devices in her bag. She spoke with Kev and Sam for another ten minutes before she headed home. Samantha said to Judy, "I really appreciate all that you have done for my dad today. He looks very happy and relaxed. It helps me too.

Jacob came over after work to spend time with her dad and Samantha. Now and then, he would spend the night with Sam to keep her company. Samantha and Jacob checked on Kevin. He was resting peacefully.

Part 5

Tim and Maggie's Split

Tim had been procrastinating about breaking up with Maggie for the last month. Maggie had become too demanding and aggressive with Tim and the rest of the family. Gigi and Bernard had been hearing more rumors about Maggie's past.

They heard from a friend who knew a friend who made comments about Maggie and her family. Some people who knew her and her brother were both believers in conspiracy theories. Their own friends and family removed themselves because of their racial and radical behaviors. They were the talk of the town.

They didn't want to get involved unless their dad asked them to intervene. Prisilla noticed that Maggie was getting too aggressive with Tim and waited for her dad to say something. She also didn't want to intervene.

She loved her dad too much. She was hoping that Tim would finally break up with Maggie. It would be in his best interest. Maggie was a known gold digger and was possibly taking advantage of Tim's kindness. Tim wasn't that easy to pull the wool over his eyes.

That was why he wanted to break up with her in front of his entire family for safety reasons. Tim never got Maggie a credit card or expensive gifts, but a Movado watch worth $150 and a pair of shoes worth $150, but nothing more than that.

His family disapproved in silence, especially his three children. Prisilla and the rest of the family didn't want to put that type of pressure on Tim. They waited for Tim to make that decision to break up with Maggie of his own accord.

Tim called his three children, Prisilla, Gigi, and Bernard, via Zoom to discuss his decision to call it quits with Maggie. They had been waiting for this for months. Even when, at one time, they said, "If you're happy, we are happy," the Kingston family then saw Maggie differently. She turned out not to be the right woman for Tim.

Tim became unhappy with Maggie after a debate about her moving in. Tim was not living with any woman like Maggie after his wife Deborah's sudden death.

Unless he was in love with Maggie, for Tim, it would be too much of a gamble and headache to continue with this woman. "It was fun while it lasted," according to Tim, and nothing else.

Tim talked to his grown kids and explained that he had no interest in Maggie because she was becoming too demanding. Tim didn't like aggressive women. Tim said to his kids that he didn't want her to move in with him because of Maggie's attitude.

They nodded their heads with approval. Individually, they said a few words to their dad. They were happy with his decision. Bernard said, "Dad, I got you."

The girls said, "Dad, I got your back." Maggie was a hard shell to break, but Tim was going to break through that shell no matter what.

His kids recommended doing it while the family was together. Gigi and Bernard were coming during their summer break for Samantha and Jacob's party.

Tim did agree to do it before the reveal party or during. It would be much easier for Tim's family to be there because of Maggie's aggressive behavior toward Tim and the rest of the Kingston family. Doable. Her behavior was atrocious.

Tim felt grateful for the feedback he received from his kids. Tim told Gigi and Bernard, "I can't wait to see you during the summer."

They said the same thing: "Can't wait."

He added that he would like to break bread with them before Samantha and Jacob's reveal party in July. They were happy to spend time together.

Tim was not going to give Maggie any inkling about breaking up. He was going to act like nothing was going on. Tim tended to have a straight face for everything. When Tim wanted to be cautious about a situation, he knew exactly what he needed to do to keep calm about saying anything to anyone.

He was contemplating. He was reevaluating his relationship with Maggie. It was one of the most important decisions he ever made in a relationship. Tim, who had no experience breaking up with a woman, might find it challenging. He lost his wife suddenly and didn't know how to disappoint a woman. Tim and Deborah had a healthy and loving relationship since they met decades ago. Yes, like every relationship, it had its ups and downs. This one would be a little different regarding Maggie.

Time will tell…

Chapter 6

Part 1
Beverly's GYN Outcome

After appearing at her GYN appointment with Dr. Alvarado to see if she did suffer from vaginal stenosis after chemo and radiation, Beverly was anxious to hear the outcome of her GYN exam.

During her call with Jonathan Sr., she told him that she was eager to make love to him after two years of not having sex. Jonathan Sr. said, "I didn't want to pressure you to have sex. I am devoted to you." He had been devoted, loyal, and faithful to Beverly and his kids. Sex has always been great with Beverly. So he had been waiting patiently till she was ready.

Prisilla was the one who saved Beverly's life, and she owed her everything for it, according to Beverly. The Decanti-Cartwright family was so humble toward Dr. Kingston. They appreciated her success in saving lives.

Dr. Prisilla Kingston recommended an extensive vaginal examination for Beverly a few weeks ago that included a cervical checkup with Dr. Alvarado.

Beverly was so excited to get additional good news after her MRI and blood work revealed that her cancer cells had shrunk drastically.

Dr. Alvarado, a gynecologist who had twenty years of experience in gynecological and women's health, was overseeing Beverly's exams.

Beverly sat down with Dr. Alvarado to discuss the results.

Beverly was ready to hear the news—any news. Dr. Alvarado greeted Beverly with a friendly smile and said she had exciting news for Beverly.

Beverly couldn't stay still. She was too excited. Dr. Alvarado said, "I would like to discuss your results in detail."

Both reviewed the results together. Dr. Alvarado said, "Beverly, first, your vaginal depth hasn't narrowed but 1/4 of an inch, which wasn't a lot. It wouldn't be uncomfortable for you and your husband to have sex."

Beverly curiously asked during her visit, "How about the loss of vaginal depth?"

Dr. Alvarado explained, "Even if you have only that much, your husband must have an exaggerated-size penis. Second, there are no signs of any damage to the vaginal depth, cervix, or any sign of cancer in your vaginal canal." Period...Beverly had very good news for Jonathan Sr. Her mind went directly to sex, sex, and sex.

Beverly said thank you to Dr. Alvarado like ten times. She started to cry after two years of radiation and chemo. She couldn't wait to tell Jonathan Sr. the good news.

Dr. Alvarado scheduled a GYN exam in a year. It would be Beverly's second appointment with him after her first GYN doctor of twenty years retired. Beverly said she would call for the appointment. She wanted to go home to surprise Jonathan Sr. with the good news.

Dr. Alvarado smirked and said, "Go on, girl, and be with your family.

Part 2

Beverly and Jonathan Sr.'s Romantic Weekend

She rushed home to cook a nice meal for Jonathan Sr. Beverly set up the table with their best chinaware and glasses to drink wine.

She cooked his favorite meal—steak, medium rare, just the way Jonathan Sr. liked it. A cold pasta salad and freshly roasted veggies straight from the oven.

Beverly called Mrs. Daniels to pick up her kids and take them to her parents' home for a few hours.

Mrs. Daniels kind of figured out on her own that Beverly wanted to spend time with her hubby. Maybe tell Jonathan Sr. some good news. She can hear it in Beverly's voice.

So Mrs. Daniels didn't say another word. She went to pick up the kids and took Tammy, Jonathan Jr., and Genny to Beverly's parents' home.

It seemed that everyone was waiting for Beverly to share the news with them. The Descanti-Cartwright family valued their privacy; it was vital and well-protected. So they all waited, as much as Jonathan I and Yolanda waited to hear the news. Beverly had been quiet about it for a few weeks till she got the okay.

Jonathan Sr. just arrived from work. He saw his wife with the sexiest and hottest panties and bra set that he hadn't seen on her. She went and bought herself the sexiest lingerie without Jonathan Sr. knowing. She was wearing a pair of five-inch stiletto heels and garter belts that connected to the panties.

He immediately got aroused. Seeing Beverly dressed like that, he was ready to make love to her over and over again. He didn't hesitate to grab her tightly and kiss her passionately.

He felt a little embarrassed. He just arrived from work, smelling like he came from work. Beverly just looked at him with total desire. *Just go down on him like an animal in heat*, she said to herself. It's her Jonathan Sr.

He rushed and peeled off his work uniform as he was going upstairs to shower. Beverly found it intoxicating, and it turned her on. She reminded Jonathan Sr. that after all these years together, he still made her weak in the knees.

All Jonathan Sr. was thinking was how he was going to take over her in bed after two years of no sex. After eighteen years, Beverly still saw her Jonathan Sr. as hot and handsome with a built body that was worthy of holding every night. Jonathan Sr. turned and shook his penis on top of the stairs, heading to the bedroom to shower.

Beverly gushed and wanted him to hurry. She went upstairs to watch Jonathan Sr. take a shower. He was as hard as wood. She swung her beautiful curves while Jonathan Sr. grabbed his fat piece.

Jonathan Sr. hadn't had sex with Beverly, so he jerked off to make the next round even longer. Beverly got a string of balls that she stored in the bottom of the basin, washed it, dried it seductively, and placed it inside her vagina, pulling it out slowly.

It was too thrilling to cum yet. Jonathan Sr. helped her to take off her heels first. Beverly went in the shower with panties and all, just to get things going with her husband. He bent down slowly to remove Beverly's panties. Jonathan Sr. went directly to her clit and started pulling it with his lips. Gently in a circular motion, and Beverly was in ecstasy.

Jonathan Sr. jerked off and continued to satisfy his beautiful wife. But he wasn't done yet with Beverly. Beverly wasn't done satisfying her husband either.

He and Beverly got out of the shower. Jonathan Sr. just picked her up and placed her on top of the two-sided sink and basin. He looked directly at her and jammed it hard as Beverly moaned. Jonathan Sr. even got harder than before. Beverly put both of her hands against the mirror. He licked her breast, which remained perky even after chemo.

It was steamy. Jonathan Sr. wiped the mirror with a washcloth. Jonathan Sr. continued jamming his large dick inside her warm, tender canal. She just wanted to fuck him like he was the only one who could satisfy her completely—caressing it, embracing it.

She did have dinner in the oven. But she didn't care. She was getting the attention she needed from Jonathan Sr. that went on for hours.

Then they took it to the top of the stairs. He grabbed the arch of her back and held it gently so he could continue making love to his wife. Beverly was groaning at the top of the stairs while Jonathan Sr. ate her like a peach.

She said, "Yes, yes, yes!"

He said, "Baby, I waited for you patiently. Now that I have you in my arms, I don't want to let you go."

She said, "We have a long weekend to prove it," while Jonathan Sr. was banging and pounding her pussy, almost making it roar. They continued excavating the entire home, fucking and sucking from the bathroom, through hallways, in their bedroom, and yes, one time in the car, as well as near his workstation in the garage.

After Jonathan Sr. and Beverly ravished each other's bodies, they took notice about picking up the kids at their grandparents, Antonio and Sofia.

They looked at each other and said, "Oh, shit! Our kids!" They both cracked up.

Beverly said, "No, seriously, the kids."

Jonathan Sr. wrapped himself in his short robe. Beverly came down in her robe. He was about to call Sofia when Beverly suggested, "Let's leave Tammy, Jonathan Jr., and Genny with my parents over-night. Then with your parents, Jonathan I and Yolanda, for a night till Sunday afternoon.

Jonathan Sr. said, "Hell, yeah. Call Sofia if she can stay with Tammy, Jonathan Jr., and Genny."

Sofia replied, "Yes, but they don't have a night bag with their things." Beverly told her mom while Jonathan Sr. was talking to his in-law that they would prepare their night bags and take them over after they eat.

Then Beverly called Yolanda to ask the same thing about the kids staying overnight. Yolanda answered her cell phone. Beverly asked Yolanda about Tammy, Jonathan Jr., and Genny staying till Sunday afternoon.

She said, "Absolutely, we haven't spent time with those precious babies in a while. Make sure they have everything they need for their entertainment."

Beverly answered, "Of course we will. Thank you, Ma."

They prepared Tammy, Jonathan Jr., and Genny's overnight bags. Jonathan Sr. went to Beverly's parents' home to take the bags over after dinner.

Jonathan Sr. left quickly to spend quality time with the wife he loved and adored so much. Beverly was reheating the perfect meal for her man. Jonathan Sr. came in when Beverly had everything set up in the dining room. They sat down, ate, laughed, and had more sex, sex, and more sex.

They had the whole weekend alone; Jonathan Sr. was off that weekend, and they had everything they needed at home. They also made plans to get couples massages that same weekend. Everything was good to go. Everything went well according to Beverly's plan. Jonathan Sr. was nice and calm now. He had been so tense about Beverly's health. Now, he and Beverly could relax.

Part 3

Tammy, Jonathan Jr., and Genny's Weekend Stay with Jonathan I, Antonio, Yolanda, and Sofia

While Beverly and Jonathan Sr. were enjoying their weekend together, Sofia and Antonio, who had the energy of a forty-year-old couple, spent time with the kids, taking them to see a movie, eat, play in the park, and make strawberry gelato that Sofia would make from scratch.

It was Sofia's favorite treat for the kids. Tammy, Jonathan Jr., and Genny loved Grandma Sofia's strawberry gelato.

Sofia would make it every time she and Antonio would visit Beverly and Jonathan Sr., especially during the already hot days in Flagstaff. It would reach like 120 degrees at times. It would make everyone's day when Sofia made it.

Sofia and Antonio adored their grandchildren. Tammy, Jonathan Jr., and Genny always had a good time with their grandparents. Genny was too hyped and joked all the time. Tammy, the shy one, would roll her eyes at her sister, Genny.

Jonathan Jr. always entertained himself with video games with Grandpa Antonio.

Grandparents Sofia and Antonio spoiled those kids like they did with Beverly. Antonio always loved scaring the kids with spooky stories. Sofia would hold them close to her breasts like their lives depended on it.

They only had a short time together with the kids, so they made the most of it. The kid's grandparents always had a good time with Tammy, Jonathan Jr., and Genny too.

Sofia and Antonio washed the kids' clothes and got the kids all cleaned up. They put them in their rooms when they would come over to spend a night. They were going to Jonathan I and Yolanda's home the next day. Antonio and Sofia made sure that Jonathan I and Yolanda didn't have to lift a finger. They just spent quality time with the kids and had fun.

The next day, Antonio took Tammy, Jonathan Jr., and Genny to Jonathan I and Yolanda's home in Phoenix.

They had a beautiful Tudor-style home Jonathan I had built when Jonathan Sr. was only a year old. It had a built-in fireplace in the living room, yard, and bedroom; five bedrooms, with three and a half bathrooms; and a large yard. The kitchen was recently renovated for Yolanda as a Valentine's gift.

Once Antonio arrived, Tammy, Jonathan Jr., and Genny ran over to Yolanda, kissed her on the cheek, and went to hug Jonathan I. Yolanda offered Antonio a glass of homemade lemonade.

He said, "Yes, Mama Yolanda, I would love a glass of your homemade lemonade." Jonathan I heard Antonio come in with the kids. Genny sat next to her grandpa, Jonathan I, and whispered to him about rubbing his hair. He said, "Go ahead, sweetie."

Jonathan I offered a cigar to Antonio. He just got some Cubanos. Antonio said. "Yes, thank you." He offered a glass of high-quality cognac to Antonio. They went outside and smoked their Cubanos in the yard. Yolanda wasn't fond of the smell in the home, so Jonathan I would go out to the yard out of respect for his wife.

Yolanda has the outgoing personality and energy of a forty-year-old woman, while Jonathan I was more of a laid-back man who liked to have fun with the kids—playing video games with Jonathan Jr. for sport.

Jonathan Jr. watched sports with his grandpa when games were up for play, as did Jonathan Sr., who was an athlete in his younger days in high school. Antonio spent about an hour with Jonathan I because he had a long ride back to Flagstaff. He said goodbye to his grandbabies, Yolanda, and Jonathan I. He told them that their dad said they should behave. They responded with an okay. He headed back home.

The very next day, Tammy, Jonathan Jr., and Genny were ready to return to their parents' home. Jonathan I and Yolanda loaded them into his Ford EV and took them straight over to Jonathan Sr. and Beverly. By the time the kids got home, Beverly was waiting at the doorway.

Beverly and the kids waved to Jonathan I as he and Yolanda stood sitting in his EV, left, and went directly home.

Chapter 7

Part 1
Jeremy and Prisilla's Home Meal

Three days before Jeremy returned to Chicago, he called Prisilla to make dinner for her at Betty and Carlson's home—Jeremy's grandparents.

Prisilla didn't answer the call at first, so Jeremy left a message for Prisilla to call back during her free time. Jeremy also told Prisilla not to worry about anything and that he was hoping she could make it.

Whether he saw Prisilla before leaving or not, he got this. When he returned to Flagstaff in several weeks, he would invite her to his home to have dinner. He was hopeful.

That was how confident Jeremy was, even as a teenager. He had the confidence to achieve anything he wanted. Betty and Carlson were very proud of Jeremy's achievements in the pediatrics department and everything else in his life.

They supported whatever decisions Jeremy made because he had it in him ever since he was a little boy.

His grandparents were raised during a difficult time in the '60s. The civil rights movement propelled them to make good in their lives.

Jeremy's parents couldn't support him. His parents couldn't take care of their own son because his mom died of an apparent overdose, and his father left him alone most of the time.

Betty and Carlson Greenleaf-Keiths took Jeremy after his parents abandoned him. They took Jeremy under their wings as their own and raised him to become an outstanding and grateful man.

Betty and Carlson couldn't have children, so having Jeremy was a blessing from God.

(This entire book was fictional and not based on true facts.)

Both of their mothers died during childbirth. Betty and Carlson's great-grandparents were enslaved and became free after the Emancipation Proclamation was signed into law. Their struggles to make a life for them came at a price, but they made it.

Prisilla returned Jeremy's call two hours later. She apologized for her tardiness. She explained to Jeremy that she had some appointments with some of her patients. Jeremy said with a smile, "It's okay. I am glad you returned my call."

Not saying much on the phone, she replied, "I would love to have dinner with you and your grandparents." Jeremy told Prisilla that his grandparents were planning a spiritual retreat and spa with friends from their congregation.

Jeremy didn't know for sure, he added. He said that even if they didn't go, he would love for Prisilla to get better acquainted with his grandparents, Betty and Carlson. They spent about seven minutes on their cell phones talking before her next patient arrived.

Jeremy talked about setting it up for Thursday evening. Prisilla mentioned that was good timing. Jeremy and Prisilla were glad not to cancel this time. Before hanging up, they made an official date as a promise, and then they hung up.

The day before Jeremy left for Chicago to finish his final plan to move to Flagstaff, Betty and Carlson helped to prepare dinner for Prisilla and Jeremy. His grandparents weren't going to the retreat and spa because it was cancelled till the beginning of June.

Some of their congregation members had conflicting schedules and needed to make some changes for a later date.

Jeremy told his grandmother that they would be joining Jeremy and Prisilla for dinner. Jeremy was happy that they weren't going, so they could meet Prisilla. Whether it was before or after, Jeremy was happy, no matter what the outcome would be. He was over the moon about seeing Prisilla again before his departure from Arizona.

The day of the dinner, the vibe was electric, and the mood was somber. Jeremy didn't know that Prisilla loved soul food. Jeremy found out the day he spoke to her to invite her over for dinner.

Jeremy and Grandma Betty started to cook dinner for her husband and Jeremy's guest, Prisilla. Betty wanted to impress Prisilla, so she made her signature homemade biscuits, baked chicken with yellow rice, canned yams, salad, homemade dressings, and Prisilla's favorite dessert, blueberry goose pie.

He spoke about Prisilla with gladness. Every time Betty would say Prisilla's name, "Oh, Priscilla," he would raise his metrosexual brows and smile.

Betty asked Jeremy if he really liked this woman. He said, "Ever since the first day I laid my eyes on her during one of many medical conferences we were attending, not once but a few times." Betty always told Jeremy to find a woman, settle down, and have children.

Jeremy and Prisilla didn't have children because of their work and being in their forties.

He dated a lot, but nothing came out of it because he wasn't ready to be with one woman. On the other hand, Priscilla wanted to be financially secure and find a good man to father her children successfully.

Jeremy told Betty that Prisilla might be the one. "Are you sure she feels the same way for you, Jeremy?" said Betty.

He replied, "Yes, she does. I can feel it."

He said he'd never felt the way he did with Prisilla. She just stood surprised. Finally, Jeremy wanted to settle down.

As Carlson was walking into the kitchen, he was surprised to hear that his grandson was excited about being with a woman like Prisilla. Carlson thought Prisilla must be a phenomenal woman, and rightly so. Jeremy deserved a good woman in his life, not some tramp he had been with before meeting Prisilla.

Prisilla called while his family was in the kitchen to say that she was on her way. Jeremy said, "Okay," and told his grandparents.

The patio table was set up by Betty with candles she made and flowers that she grew in her garden. Carlson put together a mix of classic R and B, soft rock, and the latest country music. It was about 7:00 p.m. The night was crystal-clear—a nice night to eat outdoors.

The Greenleaf-Keiths's front lawn was perfectly trimmed with a wooden gate and with lights that wrapped around their home. The two-story home had four bedrooms, two and a half bathrooms, a beautiful kitchen that looked fabulous, a two-sided garage, a dozen flower beds, and a classic 1970 Benz that they both bought together from an antique dealer.

As Prisilla was let in, Jeremy introduced her to Betty, his grandma, and then to Carlson, who was sitting in his easy chair, waiting patiently to eat. The patio area was ready for everyone to head directly to it.

She said, "Everything smelled delicious, Ms. Greenleaf-Keiths."

Betty said, "Aww, thank you, Prisilla, but you can call me Betty."

Carlson said, "Prisilla, don't be nervous. We are happy to meet you. See how happy my Jeremy is!"

Jeremy waved his hands, saying quietly, "You are embarrassing me." They all laughed.

Prisilla said, "Don't worry, Jeremy. I'm glad to see you, too."

They sat, drank a few glasses of imported wine, and had dinner. They chatted, laughed at Carlson's stories about Jeremy, and continued enjoying Prisilla's company. They were having a ball, listening to music, and dancing. The Greenleaf-Keiths were singing along to the tunes that Carlson had prepared for the evening.

Prisilla and Jeremy talked about his trip back to Chicago. Prisilla talked about the value of family and close friendships. Jeremy was mesmerized by how pretty she was and how sweet she was.

Jeremy talked about his plans to ask Prisilla for another date but waited till he took her home to ask.

They kept talking, and then Betty and Carlson went to join them at the table, just for a little while longer before heading to bed for work. Late sixties and still working were by choice. They called it a night and said good night to Prisilla. She returned the pleasantry to the Greenleaf-Keiths.

They stood there talking, laughing, and sipping the last bit of wine before Jeremy drove Prisilla home.

Jeremy opened his car door and allowed Prisilla to sit in first, like his grandpa taught Jeremy when courting a woman. Jeremy hopped on and drove.

They talked during the ride about the next date, which she said yes to. He opened his car door again for Prisilla to exit. After walking side by side, he gave her a hot and steamy kiss and walked her home, where she and her dad, Tim, lived. Jeremy got into his car, waved at her, and spun off.

Prisilla called the next day to thank Jeremy for a beautiful evening with his grandparents, Betty and Carlson. He said he enjoyed spending time with her. She also added that Jeremy should have a safe flight back to Chicago. He said, "Thank you, and I will see you soon."

She reminded Jeremy to call as soon as he came back to Flagstaff. He said absolutely and headed to the airport.

Part 2

A Small Gathering for Father's Day

After the Mother's Day celebration that Victor, Charles, Kathy, and Derrick threw for the ladies, they wanted to reciprocate, but in a different way.

The men were hikers and campers. So Kathy, Janet, and Kitty gathered at Momma Josephine's home to reserve a Father's Day hiking, camping, and horseback riding tour in Seattle.

Once the ladies got together to finish the reservations, they had lunch at Momma Josephine's. She made a vegetable quiche, a potato salad, and a fruit salad bowl for Janet, Kitty, and Kathy.

They talked about having a small intimate dinner for them and the gentlemen before surprising them with the trip to Seattle.

Kathy was happy that her dad, although complicated at times, was a man with simple taste and style. He earned a lot of money with his business and was planning to open another location while saving money for a dream wedding for Kathy when she decided to wed. He was prepared for any emergency, big or small, too.

Now that Veronica was in Charles' life, along with Kathy, Francine, her kids, Bobby, and Momma Josephine, he might finally enjoy life with gusto. Things were going well for Charles and Veronica.

Veronica was planning a welcome back from college dinner with her kids, Dominick and Ashley, Charles, and Kathy, by the end of June, rain or shine.

Victor was different from Charles. Victor liked to travel with Janet at every opportunity he had. While he was a saver, he was also giving, kind, and considerate to others. Victor was smart with money, as was Janet. Victor bought cars and reinvented them. Janet was the gourmet. She made exotic cakes and pastries for different events, while Victor managed the finances and made payments for bills and baking goods for Janet.

Their gourmet shop business also did party catering for events around the USA.

The ladies planned a day out with Charles and Victor two days before Father's Day and then surprised them with their gifts.

The day came. They all surprised the men with a day out at Outback Steak House to eat. They went there to eat and exchanged surprise gifts for the men. A three-day vacation for the men to camp, hike, do horseback riding, and even fish if they wanted to bring fish back.

Charles, Victor, and Sean were the outdoorsy type, and it was their forte. This was the perfect gift for the men. They would have fun.

Charles and Victor were pulled back by the gift. It was thoughtful and a perfect gift, according to Charles and Victor. Victor decided to ask Sean Garrison to join them on their trip. Charles had never met this Sean, but the more, the merrier—more men, more fishing, and conversations about man shit.

Victor and Sean played on different baseball teams, and they hit it off. They hadn't been acquaintances for that long, but Victor found Sean to be a fun guy who liked fishing and camping. Charles was okay with Sean going.

It might be difficult for Charles because of his friendship with Victor. Sometimes Charles helped with their charity—USA Kids for Troubled Afghanistan."

Their friendship was bonded, and no one could get between their friendships, so Charles was okay with it if Victor was.

Charles and Victor's families had a fun time eating at Outback Steak House.

The men went straight home to prepare their hiking, fishing, and camping gear for their three-day Father's Day trip. Sean would have to go and ask his wife first because he didn't want to disappoint Catherine by just going. They both always say that if their plans change, they should let each other know at least two to three days in advance.

Sean was his own man. He and Catherine were considerate of each other's feelings and always planned things together as a couple. Catherine was an understanding woman who always tolerated Sean as much as he tolerated Catherine in a loving and caring way. She also understood that a man needed to do manly things. Catherine loved it when he was out with his fellas. He came back randy and ready to screw his wife.

The day came. Charles called Veronica to let her know that he was going on a trip that his mom, Momma Josephine, surprised him with. Veronica wasn't that kind of woman who hounded her man. She said, "Enjoy your trip with Victor, and I will see you when you return." She enjoyed seeing Charles have fun for a change.

Victor kissed Janet and met up with Charles. Victor called Sean to see if he was still going on the trip. He replied, "Yes. My wife is all in." Sean was going with the men. Victor was driving. Charles and Victor were putting their supplies onto the stretch RV with modern-day conveniences and drove over to pick up Sean. Sean hugged and gave his wife a long kiss and a few more pecks on the cheek, and then left with Victor and Charles.

When they came back after their three-day trip, they had a buttload of fish and souvenirs for their wives and Charles's girlfriend, Veronica, from Seattle. They showered the funk from their bodies and planned an evening with their partners (Janet, Veronica, and Catherine).

Part 3

Final Preparations for the Reveal

Jacob and Samantha had just arrived to meet Christina, the party planner at Janet and Victor's gourmet shop.

The mama-to-be had arranged an appointment with Janet Gerber to discuss how they wanted their vision to look for their baby's reveal party.

Janet had planned to close her shop an hour earlier to have a private meeting with Jacob, Samantha, and Christina without any interruptions from her customers.

While Victor was camping with Charles and Sean, Jacob, Samantha, and Christina gathered at the gourmet shop to start the party preparations for the reveal.

Samantha had specific details she shared with Janet and Christina, Josh's wife, while Jacob sat there listening. He and Sam already had everything settled between them. Both were told that they already knew what they were having—a boy. No one knew but the four of them.

Christina and Janet were asked to keep it a secret till the reveal. Samantha mentioned that they were invited to the baby's party. They would return after everything was set up at the P. Salas Country Club (fictitious name and place).

Samantha and Jacob told J and C that they had already reserved a spot two and a half months in advance at the country club for the fourth of July. "Fireworks will be part of the reveal as a background to the sex of the baby," said Samantha.

Samantha's entire family helped her financially with the rental. Sam and Jacob paid for the rest.

Christina and Janet were in awe. Christina said, "That is a great idea, Samantha and Jacob." They went on discussing the color scheme and designs to the very last detail—from gold-plated plates with bone-white tablecloths and napkins to the seating arrangements.

There were different types of appetizers, finger foods, desserts, beverages like wine and hard liquor, and the main course. Jacob had assigned two people to be inside four large teddy bear masks to reveal the sex of the baby.

There were white, black, and gold balloons; centerpieces for the Kingston and Garrison family members; memory bags especially made to take home as souvenirs; and a few other surprises that would be exposed at the reveal.

Jacob hired a photographer, DJ, and videographer for the reveal party.

The way Samantha had in mind to place everything in its rightful place was fascinating to hear her describe it to Christina and Janet.

Once everything was arranged, Christina and Jacob helped Janet close her shop around 7:35 p.m. Jacob and Samantha dropped Christina off at her home, while Janet went straight home.

Samantha asked Jacob to stop by a 7-Eleven to get ginger ale and saltine crackers. Sam asked Jacob to hurry because she was feeling a little queasy. Jacob replied, "Okay, babe."

Sam said, "Thank you, honey."

"That's perfect," Jacob said to Sam. "I can fill up our car with gas at the same time." He went in first, paid for gas, and bought a bottle of ginger ale and saltine crackers for Samantha. He handed them to her to settle her stomach.

Jacob finished filling up the car with gas, hopped in the car, and took Samantha home to rest. In the car, Sam asked Jacob if he could stay with her overnight, just in case. Jacob said, "Yes, my love. I will stay with you tonight. After I take you home, I will rush to my parents' home and pack up a few things for work."

Jacob left and came back to keep his fiancée company. Jacob loved Samantha so much that he would do anything for her.

Samantha was ready to spend the rest of her life with Jacob. Plan a wedding, possibly have another child, and buy their own home within eight years. She was confident enough for her and Jacob.

That was their goal and dream from day one—to achieve all those things as a couple.

Chapter 8

JEREMY'S LEAVING CHICAGO FOR GOOD

A Surprise Proposal for Prisilla
A Lunch Invitation for Her Dad, Tim

After three weeks of being in Chicago, Jeremy's realtor had everything done and sold the loft. Jeremy would be receiving a check within five to seven days with the asking price. He was pleased with the results of the sale.

Jeremy also got good news that his supervisor, Mr. McCaffery, had submitted his paperwork to his boss for Jeremy's transfer to Flagstaff Hospital in one week.

Jeremy had a good feeling. He was ready to settle in his new home and be next to his grandparents, Betty and Carlson, and Prisilla.

At that point, he saw that Prisilla was calling. Jeremy said quietly to himself that everything was going too fast before answering his cell. Jeremy felt great every time Prisilla called.

They hadn't spoken for close to two weeks because they were busy with work and stuff, but they did text and video calls in between being busy to see how they were doing. They always thought of each other. They just didn't want to sound desperate when they spoke on the cell. Deep inside, they missed each other and couldn't wait to be together.

Jeremy didn't say much, not to spoil the surprise. He mentioned that everything was in the works and that things were going well for him. They exchanged pleasantries with each other.

They seemed anxious during their calls, so they decided to do a video chat later in the evening. They said they would see each other soon and hung up to finish their work.

Only a few knew that Prisilla and Jeremy were together as friends but not as a couple. That hadn't been established yet.

He planned to ask Prisilla to invite her dad, Tim, to meet over lunch upon his return to Arizona. He would rather wait to ask during the video chat, or he would wait until he got to Flagstaff and then ask Prisilla to invite her dad for lunch or dinner.

A couple of hours passed. Jeremy sent a video invite to Prisilla. They only texted each other. This was the right time to speak, so they could look at each other directly.

He hadn't seen Prisilla in person since his return to Chicago. Prisilla felt the same way on her end.

Once the video chat started, Jeremy and Prisilla threw a kiss and laughed. While they were talking, Jeremy was building his confidence to ask her to go out to eat with him and her dad, Tim.

So he asked. Prisilla said, "Of course. I always talk about you. My dad wants to meet you because he thinks you aren't real."

Jeremy asked, "Why?"

Prisilla said, "Because I say too many nice things about you, and he wanted to see it for himself."

He said, "Okay."

Jeremy asked Prisilla about Giovanni's and Sons Restaurant and Bar, which she had been raving about. He also asked, "Does the restaurant accept reservations only?"

She said, "Yes, they do and allow walk-ins too at Giovanni's and Sons. Reservations are much better."

Jeremy said, "Great. Can we plan it when I return to Arizona?"

She responded, "Absolutely."

Prisilla said, "I will remind my dad to look at his schedule, and I will work around mine."

Jeremy said, "That sounds like a plan."

They talked for another hour, then said goodnight.

Two weeks later, Jeremy returned to Flagstaff. He went to the Kingston private medical practice. He asked the front desk receptionist to tell Prisilla to come to the front desk.

When she came to the front area to talk to the receptionist, Jeremy secretly surprised Prisilla with flowers, candies, and a card with a friendship message in it.

She stood there in shock.

Prisilla did remember giving Jeremy the address when he was in Flagstaff. Jeremy hoped that she didn't freak out when she saw him, but it was the contrary. Prisilla was not only shocked but was excited to finally see Jeremy again.

They gave a kiss and a big, humongous hug that lasted about two minutes. Prisilla looked at her receptionist and smiled. She whispered, "Thank you," and kept hugging Jeremy.

He mentioned that he needed to run some errands. Jeremy told Prisilla that he would call her in her free time. She said to call around 8:00 p.m. He accepted.

Immediately, Prisilla made the reservations for her, Tim, and Jeremy for Sunday night. She waited for Jeremy's call to let him know.

For the rest of the day, they were thinking about each other.

It was 8:00 p.m. She was on her PC looking over some bloodwork of her patients when Jeremy called.

She answered and started her conversation with Jeremy about the reservations. He was waiting for a response from Prisilla.

She mentioned that her dad, Tim, would be accepting his invitation with pleasure. "My dad wants to meet you on Sunday night at Giovanni's and Sons."

Jeremy said, "Can't wait so he can see that I am real."

Prisilla laughed so hard that Jeremy found it sexy. Prisilla had the voice of a songbird. They were really into each other, and it showed. Their attraction to each other was profoundly deep and real.

He could see himself possibly marrying Prisilla. Prisilla already imagined herself in a wedding dress. Ever since she was sixteen years old, she dreamed of being with a man whom she could love, care for, and be faithful to.

Jeremy's past relationships with women ended in nothing, but with Prisilla, he saw himself falling for her.

While they were thinking about all the possibilities of being a couple, they talked in between their thoughts.

It went on until 10:00 p.m., and they weren't ready to hang up, but it was getting late. They talked for another three minutes, and then they said goodnight like the previous night.

Sunday was fast approaching. Jeremy would wear a tie, shirt, and dress pants. Prisilla was going to wear a green dress, heels, and a blazer. She asked her dad to wear a tie, loafers, and slacks because Jeremy would be getting dressed in business casual.

Tim said, "No problem. Where are we going?"

She said, "To Giovanni's."

Her dad said, "Fantastic. I like Giovanni's."

They all called it a night.

Jeremy was getting ready for the evening out with Prisilla and Tim. Jeremy was thinking that popping the question to Prisilla in front of Mr. Tim Kingston was nerve-wracking. He had to take a deep breath just to get his mind straight.

Prisilla and her dad were getting ready to meet with Jeremy at Giovanni's and Sons. Their dinner reservation at Giovanni's is at 7:20 p.m. Prisilla was super nervous that her dad would finally meet Jeremy for the first time. She was sure that Tim would like Jeremy and had high expectations that they would get along.

Individually, they got in their cars to meet. Tim and Prisilla arrived first at Giovanni's. The *maître d'* escorted them to their table and asked what they would like to drink. Prisilla told the *maître d'* to give them five minutes because her friend Jeremy would be joining them. The *maître d'* smiled and poured water into their glasses.

That was when Prisilla noticed Jeremy walking as handsomely as ever. They both stood up from their chairs and greeted Jeremy as he approached the table.

He apologized for his tardiness. She said, "We just got here for like three minutes, so you are right on time." Prisilla introduced Jeremy to her dad. He said, "Nice to meet you," and they started their evening.

They talked for about five minutes when the *maître d'* stopped over at their table. The *maître d'* introduced himself and told them that he would be sending a waiter to claim their meal. He said, "What would you like to drink?" Jeremy and Prisilla ordered a bottle of classic cabernet sauvignon, and her dad asked for a Scottish whiskey with a cube of ice and a lime wedge.

While they were waiting for their bottle, Tim's drink arrived. They started chatting about family, work, recreational sports, and leisure time.

The *maître d'* provided Tim's drink first, then opened the bottle of cabernet and poured the first glasses for Prisilla and Jeremy. They celebrated with a tap of the glasses.

The night was going so well. They laughed and joked around. Prisilla saw how her dad, Tim, and Jeremy were getting along so well. They had the same taste in clothes and sports and the same type of witty sense of humor. It seemed too good to be true.

Then the moment came to ask Mr. Kingston for his daughter's hand in friendship, loyalty, and engagement.

Jeremy stood there while a sweat bead was streaming down his face. Tim asked, "Are you okay, son?"

Jeremy returned to Tim and said, "I'm okay. Just a little nervous with what I am about to ask." Prisilla's hands were fidgeting like she was expecting a surprise from Jeremy.

Tim said, you can tell me, and smiled. He liked Jeremy like he knew him for a while because of what Prisilla was saying about Jeremy.

Jeremy cleared his voice and said, "Mr. Kingston. I've grown very fond of your daughter, Prisilla. My days in Chicago only ended with me missing Prisilla. There is nothing that I wouldn't do to keep Prisilla happy and be the man who would care for, cherish, and love her for a lifetime."

Tim said jokingly, "Stop!" Jeremy and Prisilla didn't know how to react. Then Tim said, "You can call me Papa Tim." And both exhaled.

Jeremy continued, "Prisilla, I'm not asking you to say yes right now. I will hold on to this." Then he showed off a 5-carat ring to both. Tim and Prisilla looked like they were about to burst off their chairs. That wasn't the case. Jeremy went on saying, "Prisilla, I will hold the ring for a year till you decide, and if you say no, our friendship and bond are unbreakable."

Tim said, "I love this guy. Prisilla, if you don't say yes, I will."

They all laughed, and even the other guests laughed at Giovanni's.

Everyone was waiting desperately to hear an answer from Prisilla. She couldn't say no to that. Her dad looked with approval and appreciation at Jeremy's having the guts to ask.

He had been waiting for Prisilla to finally settle down, and Jeremy was the one. Tim and Jeremy looked at each other when Prisilla screamed and said, "I don't want to wait a year! I want to say yes tonight!" The guests clapped as they watched Jeremy place the flawless ring on Prisilla's finger.

Tim was overjoyed that Prisilla had found a good man, and she looked beyond the color of his skin. Tim already knew how beautiful their kids would look if they did.

The night was the best night that they had had in a long time. They continued their night at Giovanni's. Tim sat there with a smile on his face while watching Jeremy and Prisilla dance near the piano.

They ended up being the last to exit Giovanni's and Sons. They were heading to their cars. Before that, Tim took Jeremy's hands, held them for a moment, and said, "I am happy to include you in our family. My daughter talked about you with good reason. I must admit. I thought you weren't a real person because of Prisilla's track record of a few relationships that were doomed to fail.

Jeremy assured him that it would be different for Prisilla. He added, "Between you and me, I love Prisilla already, but please don't tell her." The conversation with Jeremy ended. Tim went to his car to sit there.

They said to one another, "Don't hesitate to call me." They arrived home about or close to 11:00 p.m. safe and sound.

Prisilla and her dad talked till 1:00 a.m. They talked about the evening and that 5-carat ring Jeremy placed on Prisilla's finger.

The next morning, Prisilla called Jeremy to ask if he would be honored to attend her cousin Samantha and her fiancé Jacob's reveal party on July 4. Jeremy said, "Wherever you go, love, I would be honored to go too."

They went on talking for a few more minutes. Jeremy was still organizing his new home. Tim was closing their private practice for the day to attend to two patients alongside Prisilla at the main hospital.

Now it was official. Prisilla's first day of being engaged to Jeremy was worth talking about with her colleagues. But she didn't have to. It showed because it was so shiny and brilliant enough that everyone could see it from three feet away.

It was a beautiful day for Prisilla.

Chapter 9

SAMANTHA AND JACOB'S BABY REVEAL PARTY HAS COME

Tim's younger adult children, Gigi and Bernard, just arrived from college. The whole summer with their entire family in Flagstaff was always full of excitement.

Tim was extremely thrilled that all his kids would be together this time since New Year's Eve 2022. Bernard would be graduating from college in 2024 with a master's in medical technical engineering.

Bernard's sister, Gigi, would be graduating the following year with a master's in health care administration. They lived on through tradition and family values.

Around 4:45 p.m., the Kingstons and the Garrisons gathered at Tim's home.

Everything was set up at P. Salas Country Club the day earlier. Semiformal white and gold attire only was allowed, and no jeans or sneakers were allowed. Jacob provided everyone with an itinerary to follow in detail—how the night would go.

The photographer and videographer would be taking all the photos and videos. The DJ would start playing the music at the start of the reveal. Right then, the club was playing soft music in the background. The rest of the attendees could take pictures with their own phones to experience the beautiful memories at the reveal.

Between 6:00 and 7:00 p.m., drinks and appetizers would be served in the lounge area with soft music in the background.

Between 7:00 and 8:00 p.m., the baby's sex would be revealed.

Between 8:00 and 9:00 p.m., the main course with dessert would be served.

And between 9:00 and 11:00 p.m., there would be dancing, a congratulatory song for Samantha and Jacob, and fireworks.

Tim's kids asked about Maggie. He said, "We broke up. She had already been dating two other men secretly behind my back. So there is no need to worry moving forward. Maggie is history." Prisilla, Bernard, and Gigi were glad that it was over. Ahead of their cousin's reveal party, Gigi said to her dad, "At least, you didn't have to do it in front of the guests."

"No drama, no embarrassment, right," said Bernard.

Samantha was getting ready for the most exciting moment of her life. She was so overwhelmed that Jacob remained by her side to keep her calm and comfort her.

Samantha and Jacob came down the stairs, and everyone lost it. She looked so radiant and pregnant. Jacob was holding Samantha's hand and smiling. She was in her fifth month of pregnancy.

Her dad, Kevin, just stood there staring at her, with so much love in his eyes that he started to get a little weepy. Tim handed over to his brother, Kevin, a handkerchief to wipe his tears. Kevin kept saying, "My first grandbaby," over and over.

Kevin was doing well with his adjusted treatment. He was recognizing his family but still not remembering others as close guests. Kevin was alert and calm. Things seemed to be going in the right direction for Kevin and his treatment for onset dementia.

At 5:15 p.m., the Kinston and Garrison families headed toward the country club. They were the first to arrive to make sure everything would go as planned.

Other guests should be there by 6:00 p.m. promptly. Samantha mentioned to her uncle, Tim, that the attendees should be there on time. She also said, "You can escort them to the lounge area to mingle, have some drinks, and enjoy the appetizers."

People started trickling in and parking their cars. The guests waited for a few minutes, while the Kingstons and Garrisons were the first to enter the venue. At 6:01 p.m., Tim and Sean escorted the guests to the lounge area for drinks and appetizers. Family, friends, and classmates were kissing each other on the cheek, hugging, and shaking hands. Most hadn't seen each other physically in months or even a couple of years.

The guests were catching up. Waiters started bringing the appetizers over to the guests in the lounge and ordering drinks from the free open bar.

Samantha and Jacob waved as they were going into a closed area to check on the table and chair arrangements, just like Samantha had ordered as part of the rental at P. Salas.

The black, white, and gold balloons hung from corner to corner, and seven small glass candles were around each table. Super high chandeliers hung over the tables, with white tablecloths, gold plates, water-filled glasses with a lime wedge, and utensils from the country club. The place looked just perfect.

In each corner of the dining area, there were four giant boxes with black and white ribbons wrapped around them. Two women and two men would be wearing giant bear masks in formal wear, sitting in chairs, and posing like statues. Then they would change into a different pose every fifteen minutes or less.

There would be two poppers on both sides of the room with blue confetti inside. It would reveal the sex of Samantha and Jacob's baby.

There was a comfy love seat nestled with calla lilies and a slot box where the guests could put envelopes of money in for Samantha and Jacob. One popper with confetti was near Samantha and Jacob's love seat, and the other was near the DJ booth.

It was close to 7:00 p.m., and Jacob took a moment to let his dad, Sean, Samantha's dad, Kevin, Tim, and the guests head to the main dining area to sit at their assigned tables.

The moment had come. Tim and Sean directed the guests to enter the area and go to their assigned tables. The guests were looking at all the decorations. All the guests were flabbergasted. It looked so beautiful and well put together. Everyone was impressed as they walked in.

Both the Kingston and Garrison families looked so happy for Jacob and Samantha.

When everyone had taken their seats, the DJ called Samantha and Jacob, and everyone turned up the noise with whistles and loud claps.

As the DJ was playing, Prisilla, Jeremy, Christina, Josh, Janet, and Victor arrived almost simultaneously.

Prisilla went around, introducing her new beau to every family member and friend who was there. Gigi and Bernard were crazy thrilled for Prisilla, Jeremy, and that 5-carat ring that everybody noticed. "It is about Samantha and Jacob," Prisilla said to Jeremy. He agreed. The guests greeted Samantha and Jacob one by one with envelopes with money for them. They were kissing Samantha on the cheek. Some shook hands, and others were hugging them. They were happy that everyone showed up for them—all fifty guests.

Then, at 7:25 p.m., Samantha and Jacob went to the center of the dance floor and talked about how happy they were to see their family, close friends, and classmates all together in one room.

The guests giggled, whispered, and clapped.

Samantha announced, "Are you ready for the reveal?"

Everyone said, "Yesss!"

Jacob repeated, "Are you ready for the reveal?"

Everyone said, "Yesss!"

Electronically, the poppers shot out blue confetti, and everyone went up. There was such a loud roar that Samantha had to cover her ears, and Jacob held her in awe. Jacob said, "Baby, that noise is for our baby boy." Samantha started to cry because of all the love coming from all the guests at the reveal.

It was love in the air. The photographer with a snap of the camera taking photos, the videographer taking videos of every tender moment, the loud claps that filled the entire room, and the whistles from the attendees were all caught on film.

Everything had gone just the way Samantha wanted.

Then the DJ cut off the music for a minute to let everyone know that they could head to the full self-service tables to get their food by 8:00 p.m. to 9:00 p.m. The guests lined up to get their meals.

The food smelled delicious. There were chicken parm, baked ziti, garlic bread, potato and macaroni salads, steamed fish, mashed potatoes, a variety of cold salads, and salad dressings of their choice. People chatted about the food in good spirits.

The DJ continued playing music while everyone was getting their meals. The reveal party was spectacular and astounding. Everyone was having a good time, and the dancing hadn't even started. Samantha talked to the manager about having someone clean up the confetti before the dance portion started at 9:00 p.m.

People were admiring the four people with giant bear masks changing poses. Some of the guests took pictures on their phones, saying, "Samantha is so creative."

"Best idea I have seen since the last reveal party I attended," one of the guests said to her classmate.

After all the guests finished eating their meals, the waiters picked up all the plates except the glasses, just in case the guests wanted to drink more water.

Now the DJ announced that if anyone wanted to dance, they could turn up the party. The first song was house music. People got up and headed to the dance floor.

For the next two hours, people danced. Guests were mingling and having a great time.

Their immediate family took Samantha and Jacob to the middle of the floor and made a circle around them.

Samantha and Jacob were looking into each other's eyes. You could see the love between them. Samantha's eyes were gleaming with joy, and Jacob rested her head on his shoulder.

The photographer took that picture at the right time. Samantha's head on Jacob's shoulder looked very intimate and sweet. Everyone just stretched the circle a little wider so the videographer and photographer could capture the moment.

Then came the fireworks. The guests headed toward the balconies overlooking the waterfall to stare at the fireworks. They were fabulous as a backdrop.

At 10:50 p.m., the fireworks ended. Samantha announced that it was almost time to exit the country club and thanked everyone for coming. Jacob thanked everyone for coming and thanked them for their gifts (money).

As the guests were leaving, they congratulated Sam and Jacob once again.

Both dads, Kevin and Sean, stood beside Samantha and Jacob. The men kissed Samantha on the cheek. Both men shook hands with Jacob over the shoulder tap.

The Kingstons and Garrisons left last after everyone had headed home.

On the way back, both families were exhausted after the reveal and headed straight home to relax.

The next day, every guest called to say how much fun they had and to congratulate them again. That was a night to remember, especially for the Kingston-Garrison family.

Chapter 10

EIGHT YEARS LATER— FAMILIES' TRIUMPHS, PASSING, AND SUCCESSES

Eight years had passed since Samantha and Jacob's reveal party. Kevin had saved $100,000 for an exquisite wedding extravaganza for his daughter and Jacob. However, one and a half years later, after the reveal, Samantha and Jacob had decided to celebrate an intimate small "shotgun wedding" among family, close friends, and classmates who were witnesses to Sam and Jacob's wedding. After Samantha and Jacob were married, Kevin granted their wish by putting the money into something more useful—a home of their own.

Kevin gave the money to Samantha and Jacob as a wedding gift. Sam and Jacob put a down payment on the house of their dreams two years after their marriage. They were now living in it.

What Samantha and Jacob had mapped in their minds eight years ago had been finally realized. The Kingston-Garrison family got everything they wanted—marriage, kids, and a home.

They named their son Kevin Sean Michael Kingston-Garrison, who had now turned eight. Samantha returned to work with her family's private practice.

Jacob was promoted after over ten years of being in the force, from officer to detective/lieutenant at the local police station in Flagstaff. He quickly moved up in the ranks with six commendations and two awards for bravery.

Samantha and Jacob were expecting their second child eight months from now. They were planning to have another reveal party, just not as big as the last one. They already had a name for their little girl. Her name would be Catherine Annette, after Jacob's mom and Samantha's mom. Annette, Kevin's wife, was twelve years his senior before she passed away in May 2020.

Jacob's parents, Sean and Catherine, filed for separation for inconsolable differences. They needed space in between them to attend couples counseling to reconcile.

Jacob didn't know to what extent his parents' troubles in their thirty-year marriage were, especially not at that length. Jacob found out from his mom that his dad made some bad investments, and that was why they needed a break.

Jacob reminded himself that his responsibility was to his wife, Samantha, Kevin Sean Michael, and their unborn child, Catherine Annette.

He loved his parents, but they were on their own with their issues. He was happy with his life. Jacob's main concern was his own family. "My parents are grown-ups," he said.

After years of practicing oncology, the Kingston family—Tim, Prisilla, Samantha, Kevin, Gigi, and Bernard—widened their family medical practice. Tim, Kevin, and Prisilla bought a store next to their medical practice that had been empty for five years. They renovated and added offices for their new medical staff, and now it had expanded into a multiservice medical establishment.

Kevin was seventy and was thriving with the new treatment that Dr. Benning prescribed. Kevin was able to return to work—a recommendation that Dr. Benning planned for Kevin's medical treatment. It was showing tremendous results in his cognitive behavior. His desire to return to work was on his mind for a while.

When CRN Judy was to work for the Kingstons for four weeks, it turned out that she stayed working with Kevin for seven and a half years.

CRN Judy Velez continued working with Kevin and his medical care. CRN Judy Velez was promoted to supervisor of nursing. Another nurse was then attending to Kevin's medication adherence. CRN Velez came to visit Kevin at least two days a week to check on him. Her kids, Jessica and Ally, were all grown up, out of college, and with kids of their own. CRN Velez had five grandchildren, ages four to ten. Jessica had one child before she went to college. Sebastian was about 10 years old then.

Jeremy and Prisilla were meant to spend the rest of their lives together after his proposal to her seven years and ten months ago at Giovanni's and Sons.

There were some roadblocks in between with regard to their work. They would travel for work separately out of the US as part of their medical training. Jeremy's and Prisilla's schedules were a little hectic, so they had to postpone their wedding two times in five years.

Then, in August 2026, Jeremy's granddad, Carlson, age eighty, passed away of complications after getting the flu. He passed away quietly at home with his wife, Betty, their family that came from Chicago, close friends, and their congregation.

All the Kingstons and Garrisons joined a sixteen-car precession for Carlson's burial.

Jeremy got very depressed after Carlson passed but went on with his life with Grandma Betty, Prisilla, and work.

Prisilla and Betty were his rock during his struggle with depression. He would've been lost without them.

So, in 2028, Jeremy and Prisilla had the surprise grand wedding of the year on his granddad Carlson's birthday. Betty's grandniece stayed for three months in Flagstaff to help Betty around the house and with her daily travels.

It was hard for Betty, at times, after being married to Carlson for over sixty years. She had dreams about Carlson on different occasions. Jeremy was her only son. She kept him very close to her heart. That was the reason why Jeremy wanted his Granma Betty to move in to be closer, even if Betty's home was only four houses down.

Eventually, Betty sold her home to a family of six from Tulsa. Her grandniece Kenya moved back to Chicago to be with her boyfriend, and Betty moved in with Prisilla and Jeremy to their home.

To their surprise, Prisilla was pregnant at the age of forty-seven with her first child with Jeremy. Prisilla found out on their wedding day. Jeremy and Prisilla were in the process of adopting two kids, ages three and five, from Louisiana.

After eight years of their relationship, they were ecstatic. Their adoption papers went through a few months ago. The Kingston-Keiths would be an instant family almost overnight.

Christina's party planning business was booming. Josh gave Charles five weeks' notice in advance that he and his wife bought a townhouse in the most expensive real estate area in Washington, DC. "So that Christina and I could open two locations—one in Washington, DC, and one in Miami," he said.

Charles knew about moving forward, so he gave Josh his blessing as a worthy hard worker and being friendly to customers.

Josh would be traveling back and forth to help Victor and Janet with their foundation, "USA Kids in Trouble Afghanistan."

Josh hired his sister and niece, Bethany and Jayla, to run Christina and Josh's party planning store in Flagstaff while they settled in Washington, DC.

Christina taught Bethany and Jayla everything about running her business, like clockwork.

Victor and Charles planned a "farewell party" for Josh and his wife before they moved to Washington, DC. It was a profound moment. Charles was thrilled for Josh, but he would miss his favorite worker and best friend a lot. So would Janet and Victor, because they were good friends for twenty-eight years.

Josh recommended Charles to a good friend of his who had ten years of experience in auto parts. Charles was skeptical but was okay with interviewing his good friend, Gregory.

Christina and Josh were ready to embark on a new and exciting endeavor. Three months later, they moved from Flagstaff in their midthirties and started a ten-year plan to have children, put them in good schools (whether private or not), and keep their business up and running.

Three years before, Charles started helping Victor and Janet in his spare time with their foundation, running his two auto parts businesses, including his martial arts teachings. Charles's new auto parts shop business has been bringing in good revenue each year since its opening.

People came from around the state of Arizona. Victor and Janet's annual fundraiser brought people from outer states, like Nevada, to attend their gala. It continued doing good work for military families who lost loved ones on behalf of Victor and Janet's foundation.

Charles and Veronica's romance had been heating up for the past eight and a half years. They also had an intimate ceremony with family and friends. They had many dinners at home with Veronica's kids, Dominick and Ashley, when they were in town. Charles's daughter, Kathy, and Derrick hung out with Ashley and Dominick after graduating from college. Ashley graduated right after Dominick. Kathy was older than Dominick and Ashley. They got along well as a family.

They traveled and camped. They went swimming and played volleyball together when they would go on vacations to Cabo and Hawaii.

After Dominick graduated from college, he started working as a microbiologist, and Ashley started working at the main hospital as a quality assurance specialist.

Kathy and two other students, Susan and Stephanie, graduated with top honors as supervising registered nurses. Kathy continued working at PP. The other ladies were at a different location.

But in February 2027, Momma Josephine, eighty-five, passed away of natural causes. Francine and Bobby asked for bereavement to attend the funeral.

In her early years, her parents taught Momma Josephine about gentility, respect, and family values. Momma Josephine's parents were from a middle-class family that came from Georgia. They owned a small textile company before their passing.

Her twins, Barry and Billy, were then seventeen, and they were very smart kids. They skipped a grade or two, heading to college in the spring of 2029. Billy and Barry were inseparable.

Francine and Bobby had been together for more than thirteen years and had just bought a new home, so the boys had their own rooms when they came to visit.

It was a sad moment for the Villanueva family. For Cindy and Johan, Momma Josephine's siblings, it was especially hard. She became the matriarch of the family after the death of Cody.

Now that she had gone to the angels in the sky, the family went on with their lives. Charles and the rest of the family only had many great memories of the insatiable but wonderful and lovable human being, Momma Josephine. Momma Josephine lived on through her family.

Kathy and Derrick finally decided to become a couple. Derrick relocated to Flagstaff to continue his work as a corporate attorney. Kathy was elated when Derrick decided to come back home to Arizona. Kathy and Derick got engaged in the fall of 2026, and five months later, they got hitched at a wonderful wedding venue with family and friends. They rented a small home till they had saved for their own home.

Once they had enough money saved, their family would help finish paying for their home. Charles, Victor, and Janet were eager for Kathy and Derrick to give them grandbabies. It was a long time coming.

Derrick and Kathy ended up having twin girls, Pamela and Patricia, and a newborn named Derrick James.

Victor and Janet's gourmet shop had gone viral on social media, thanks to her son, Derrick, for helping them build their brand beyond Arizona. Victor and Janet were thinking of opening a new shop in the future.

Years had gone by since Beverly's bout with stage two breast cancer ten years earlier, but Beverly still saw Dr. Prisilla Kingston for her annual checkup. There had been no new signs of any kind of cancer since her first diagnosis.

Beverly had become a mentor to other women who were either struggling with having cancer or newly diagnosed, supporting and networking with other women who had been cured of breast, cervical, and uterine cancers.

Beverly and a group of women had joined forces for an annual walk marathon for cancer survivors and newly diagnosed cancer patients in Arizona.

Dr. Prisilla Kingston joined the ladies in their effort to talk about annual breast exams, screening, and women's health. Prisilla attended the walk marathon with Beverly every year.

The Kingston family was very proud of their children. Matthew got married to his college sweetheart, Arianna Valentino. Matthew and Arianna just recently had a son named Matthew Jonathan Jr. After graduating from the class of 2025, he was then working as a copilot for an international company and traveled all around the world with his wife and son on some occasions.

They had been to China, Italy, Egypt, and France within three years.

They lived near the San Francisco Bay area in a single-family home with three and a half bedrooms, one and a half bathrooms, a kitchen, a large living room, and a backyard for family gatherings. Each home had a newly installed barbeque pit and patio included in the amenities.

Jennifer was still dating and had no plans to settle down till she saved enough money to raise her kids in an environment filled with love and appreciation like her dad and mom taught their kids.

Then she met a guy who came from a family of real estate brokers in California. She told her mom, "I am dating a man who is kind, charming, and super handsome. His name is Michael McCarthy, and he wants to finally meet you and the rest of the family."

Jennifer told her mom that they were planning to visit them during the Thanksgiving weekend. She added that she would be spending Christmas with her family and the New Year with Michael's family. Beverly was concerned, but Jennifer assured her mom that she had been dating Michael for two years and they had become exclusive.

Beverly said to Jennifer, "Well, you need to talk to your dad about Michael first. You know how protective your dad is with his girls."

Jennifer replied, "I know. I'll give Daddy a call before introducing Michael to him."

Tammy, who was then twenty-two, just finished getting her degree in business, just like her brother Matthew. She was pursuing opening a yoga and meditation apparel store with her bisexual roommates. She came out to Matthew and Jennifer but didn't tell her parents yet that she was also bisexual.

Her hesitation did not allow her to say anything but to Matthew and Jennifer. Jennifer reminded Tammy, "You know how open-minded and accepting our parents are. They gave us opportunities to be ourselves and be honest with what we wanted. Our family is warm, loving, and caring. I don't think it would only matter that you are happy with your life and your achievements, especially with Daddy. I don't think they would disown you, so don't worry."

Tammy said, "Okay, I will tell them when I visit."

Tammy told her siblings that she would come out to her parents around Christmas time.

Jonathan Jr., then eighteen, wanted to go to MIT after graduating from high school to become an IT specialist. Because of his love of fixing and applying applications and design to devices and other gadgets, it was perfect for Jonathan Jr., according to his parents. His parents were all for it because Jonathan Jr. knew a lot about technology.

Beverly and Jonathan Sr. couldn't be prouder of their children's accomplishments.

Genny, who was then sixteen, wanted to be a comedian or fashion designer. She told her parents that when she finished high school, she wanted to go to FIT in New York City.

Her dad, Jonathan Sr., said to Genny a few weeks ago, "You are smart, have an eye for fashion, and have been extremely funny ever since you were a little girl. You can do anything you set your mind to do because of your drive and determination."

Sofia and Antonio had retired. They were enjoying life like it was their last. Antonio, as a birthday gift, lavished Sofia with new clothes and trips. They had traveled to France, Japan, and their beloved town of Palermo, as well as Spain, Apricale, and Campania in Italy.

Sofia had been struggling with nerve damage to her right leg. She was seeing her medical doctor for updates and medication. She was doing better with treatment. Antonio was always on top of things. His memory was long, and so was Sofia. They were in their late eighties and still had the stamina of forty-year-olds.

Antonio had built a basketball court in their backyard to play with his friends. Sofia had tea party get-togethers with her besties, laughing and telling old stories about their childhoods.

Antonio had cataracts a few years ago. Antonio had surgery because Sofia pushed him to get it done, and he was doing well. He hardly used glasses, only for reading.

Jonathan I suffered from lung disease from smoking cigars. One specialist told him that if he didn't stop smoking, he wouldn't survive another year. That was seven years ago.

Beverly helped Jonathan I seek consultation with Dr. Tim Kingston. Bev said, "He was one of the best oncologists in town. Maybe he can refer you to someone he knows." Jonathan I listened to Beverly. He even listened to Jonathan Sr. His wife, Yolanda, advised him to see Dr. Tim Kingston. "Make an appointment with Dr. T. Kingston today. The Kingston family helped Beverly get cured. Dr. Kingston can help you too," she said. Jonathan I conceded and called.

Yolanda had just retired after fifty-five years of working as a superintendent. Jonathan I retired a few years ago because he was having trouble breathing.

He made sure that his son followed in his footsteps as a dad and a provider for his children. Jonathan I was seeing Dr. T. Kingston for direction and advice.

They were all still having the best years of their lives.

Mrs. Daniels retired a year ago and was enjoying her time with Robert and Jacklyn. Robert was then a childcare development specialist at a day care center, following in his mom's footsteps. Jacklyn was then a criminal attorney at Superior Court. Jacklyn was married to another attorney and had two children, Nathaniel Jr. and Casey, like Jacklyn's mom.

They spent a lot of quality time on their off days. She was so content with all she had done for her children and that she had become as successful as she did. She could finally celebrate her life with the hobbies she always wanted to do, like selling baked goods in her spare time.

Jonathan Sr. and the rest of the family were Beverly's biggest champions; they stood strong and proud and remained by her side through it all.

Her morning rituals hadn't changed. She still jogged, ran, and meditated. She invited her fellow sisters, who survived breast cancer, to meditate in her yard.

Jonathan Sr. built a serenity and Zen area in the yard for her and her friends. He supported Beverly's endeavors and goals; he even meditated with Beverly after work.

Through Beverly's recovery, accomplishments, and strength, she has become a pillar to her peers since the first day she spoke about being a cancer survivor.

Her story touched many lives in her circle of friends. Beverly was an inspiration for breast cancer and women's health.

Even though this entire book was a fictional story, it could ring true in someone's family, neighbor, or friend's life.

About the Author

Angie Milan-Cruz came from a large family that provided her and her siblings with love and food at the table every night. Even if they experienced any hardship, they relied on faith and trust—that life's circumstances they endured were only temporary.

Her mom's inspiring words provided her and her siblings with the ability to become successful if they put their minds into it. She overcame many obstacles in life. It was writing that helped her become a writer or future published author.